The Great Barn of 1425–27
at Harmondsworth, Middlesex

The Great Barn of 1425–27 at Harmondsworth, Middlesex

Edward Impey

with Daniel Miles and Richard Lea

Historic England

Published by Historic England, The Engine House, Fire Fly Avenue, Swindon SN2 2EH
www.HistoricEngland.org.uk

First published 2017

ISBN 978-1-84802-371-0

British Library Cataloguing in Publication data
A CIP catalogue record for this book is available from the British Library.

For more information about images from the Archive, contact Archives Services Team, Historic
England, The Engine House, Fire Fly Avenue, Swindon SN2 2EH; telephone (01793) 414600.

Brought to publication by Sarah Enticknap, Publishing, Historic England.

Typeset in Georgio Pro Light 9/11pt

Edited by Liz Nichols with Paula Turner
Indexed by Caroline Jones, Osprey Indexing
Page layout by Pauline Hull

Printed in the UK by Gomer Press Ltd

Front cover:
Interior of Harmondsworth Great Barn. Courtesy Dr Tillman Kohnert.

Contents

Foreword

This is a fascinating book about a fascinating subject – the magnificent 190ft-long timber barn built by Winchester College in the early 15th century on their newly acquired estate at Harmondsworth, now famously in the shadow of Heathrow. Dr Impey brilliantly describes both its design and how it was built (a curious mixture of genius and incompetence), but also how it was used and managed and by whom, the farming routines it served, and how it compares in splendour to the other medieval great barns of England and the Continent.

I am very proud to be part of the organisation which secured its future in 2011, completed the colossal task of its conservation in 2014, initiated the research on which this book is based, and brought it to publication. It is the definitive study of this important building and will be an invaluable source for the on-site and on-line interpretation we offer to the public and English Heritage members. It will appeal to anyone with an interest in the Middle Ages. I hope you will find it as interesting as I have.

Sir Laurie Magnus
Chairman, Historic England

Introduction

'This is a cathedral', said the Poet Laureate, strewn with hay, clambering out of the Great Barn at Harmondsworth on a summer's day in 1973.[1] Betjeman's comparison was apt. Not only, as he added, is this one of the 'noblest medieval barns in the whole of England',[2] but a rare, moving and revealing memento of the vision and initiative of a great medieval institution, and the toil and organisation on which its success relied.

The institution in this case was Winchester College, for whom the barn was built in 1425–7 to serve the manor bought by its founder from the abbey of the Holy Trinity (later St Catherine's), just outside Rouen.[3] Its main purpose was the storage, in sheaves, of the manor's demesne cereal crops. Although lost to the college in 1543, it remained in agricultural use until the 1980s. In 2006, however, it was placed on the Heritage at Risk Register, and in 2011, with no viable future in private hands, it was bought by English Heritage. The price was £20,000, in real terms far less than its original cost,[4] but dwarfed by the £572,703 spent on repairs, completed on 19 December 2014.[5]

Coinciding with the opening of a new chapter in the building's history, this book has been informed by the preparatory work for its repair, has aided (in draft) the preparation of a Conservation Management Plan,[6] and may be of use in its future interpretation to the public. At its core is the description and discussion of the Great Barn's creation, design, fabric and architectural significance. However, the survival not only of the entire building, but of abundant documents including a telling series of medieval accounts, has made it possible to examine, in some detail, the practical processes, economics and personnel associated with using it, particularly in its first decades. It is hoped that these sections will contribute not just to the understanding of the Harmondsworth building and manor, but to the study of the purposes and management of medieval barns in general. For while excellent studies of individual buildings abound, notably those by F W B Charles, Walter Horn and Ernest Born, integrated studies of barns, the lands they served, and how they were used are less common: the promise of James Bond and John Weller's essay in this direction in 1991[7] remains largely unfulfilled, and only a handful of examples stand out, among them Julian Munby's and John Steane's work on New College's barn at Swalcliffe (Oxon), Christopher Dyer's contribution on Bredon (Worcs), Charles Higounet's on Vaulerent (Oise) and François Blary's on the estates of Châalis.[8] The best general study of English medieval barns and their use, meanwhile, remains Niall Brady's unpublished doctoral thesis of 1996.[9] This is also a field where myths abound – picturesque but unhelpful: great barns were 'tithe barns'; barns were built largely for display; particular examples are the largest, longest or oldest in England or their county – myths that need correction or qualification. Meanwhile, the growing body of dendrochronological evidence and improved understanding of historic carpentry are fast advancing our knowledge of when and how such buildings were put up, adapted and used. Finally, it is arguably the case that the importance of medieval farmbuildings – and most standing survivals are barns – has not yet been widely enough accepted as the equal of domestic, military, industrial or ecclesiastical buildings. And while, like other medieval buildings, they offer a tangible link with the people who built and worked in them, barns differ from the majority in representing the processes of production on which life and economy depended, not the consumption of its surplus.

The first sections of this book summarise the origin of the Harmondsworth estate, the college's motivation and the deliberations surrounding its purchase in

1392, and the resources it acquired. The next sets out what is known of why the Great Barn was built and why on such a scale, who was involved and what it may have cost. It then describes the fabric of the barn, the sequence of its construction, peculiarities of its carpentry and their significance, changes of plan and later modifications. The subsequent section discusses the administrative processes and personnel involved in managing and using the barn, particularly in the first half of the 15th century. The Great Barn is then considered in the context of the others in England and northern Europe, where it sits in the hierarchy of size and splendour, and the common circumstances that produced them. Final sections summarise the post-medieval history of the site, antiquarian interest in the building, and its architectural legacy.

The alien priory and its endowment

The manor of Harmondsworth, previously held by Harold Godwinson, was granted to Holy Trinity by William the Conqueror in 1069.[10] Such grants were not unusual, as enriching the monasteries of their homelands with English property was standard practice among the new aristocracy in the decades after the Conquest, and the king himself a major exponent.[11] A result of this was the creation, by the end of the 12th century, of over a hundred monastic households, mostly of foreign or 'alien' monks, normally dignified by the title of 'priory' from that of the prior at their head. Of these, as many as 25 eventually gained communities of six or more and fully developed claustral buildings – among them being Holy Trinity's priory at Blyth (Notts), endowed by Roger de Busli, Lord of Tickhill, in 1088.[12] The remainder, however, including Harmondsworth, rarely had more than two monks, had domestic buildings like secular manor houses and no conventual life in the normal sense.

The Conqueror's gift comprised Hermodesodes, 'with its church, and with everything pertaining to it, that is to say in fields, meadows, pastures, mills, waters, marshes, woods, and others bordering on this estate'.[13] Domesday gives more detail, and assessed the property at 30 hides and, at the time of the survey, an annual value of £20; interesting details include reference to a render of 1,000 eels *de piscinis*, suggesting the presence of fishponds, and a vineyard – one of only 42 mentioned in the survey.[14] Some additions to the monks' holdings were made soon after, probably first at Ruislip, six miles away in the north-west of the county, where Ernulf de Hesdin granted a hide in 1087, after the Domesday assessment but before both the Conqueror's death (September) and the donor's departure on campaign at an unknown date in the same year.[15] The manor of Tingewick, near Buckingham, valued at £10 per annum in 1086,[16] followed in *c* 1090,[17] and further rights there and at Harmondsworth in 1209.[18] In the early 13th century the monks also acquired the advowsons of St George's, Saham Toney (Norfolk)[19] and St Leonard's by Hastings (East Sussex).[20] The annual value of the Harmondsworth property itself, from where the remainder was administered, was estimated at £48 in 1291,[21] at £60 in 1293–4 (and the prior's goods there at £25).[22] In the years 1338–69 the monks thought it worthwhile to pay as much as £80 to the crown to retain control of the manor,[23] but on the eve of Winchester's acquisition the figure had reverted to 80 marks per annum (£53 6s 8d),[24] a more realistic figure and closer to the average profit of the manor of £67 5s 2d for the years for which records exist between 1394–5 and 1492–3.[25]

No details survive of the personnel and management of the manor from before the 13th century, but the remarkable custumal, datable to between *c* 1231 and 1273–5,[26] shows that by that period the demesne was managed in hand, as might be expected, by the *prepositus*, or reeve, and a *preco* (beadle), clearly a subordinate official; both were appointed by the prior, and were rewarded with relief of rent and services, and in the case of the reeve by a bushel of grain a week or meals every day at the prior's table.[27] The first named officers are Robert de Kelsey and Robert de Asschele, occurring in 1324, although technically they were *custodes* (keepers), acting on behalf of the king while the manor was in his hands, and were probably imposed on the prior by the royal administrator.[28] The demesne management system continued unchanged up to the closing years of the abbey's ownership, the last officials, now styled *ballivus* (bailiff), being Thomas atte Nasshe in 1386–7[29] and Thomas atte Rydyngge in 1388–89.[30] This was the estate, ordered and managed over three centuries by the monks of Holy Trinity, which the Great Barn was later built to serve and which largely funded its construction.

Wykeham's purchase

Acquisition

Although built more than 20 years after his death, the origins of the great barn lie in the activities and initiative of William of Wykeham (1324–1404), holder of high office under Edward III and Richard II, Bishop of Winchester 1366–1404, and a major figure, by any standards, in English medieval history.[31] Today, however, it is as the founder of New College at Oxford and St Mary's, Winchester (Winchester College), in response to a crisis in the recruitment and quality of the secular clergy, that Wykeham is best known.[32] Informal arrangements for teaching were in place by 1371 in Oxford and 1373 in Winchester,[33] but Wykeham knew that permanent provision could only be guaranteed by an independently endowed institution.[34] In the process of assembling the New College endowment, Wykeham lit upon the English lands of the French monasteries, long of little value to their owners thanks to repeated confiscation during Anglo-French hostilities, and so potentially available.[35] In addition, as ecclesiastical property, alien estates could be acquired relatively unhindered by the Statutes of Mortmain (1279 and 1290) on the acquisition of secular property by perpetual institutions.[36] Encouraged by these considerations, Wykeham obtained the Pope's permission to acquire such property as early as 1371, and in 1372 bought the English holdings of the priory of Mortain in Normandy (Manche), a cell of Marmoutier (Indre et Loire), to support his Oxford venture,[37] and in June 1390 he revived the tactic to supplement both the Oxford and Winchester endowments.[38] By 1388 negotiations had begun with Holy Trinity in respect of all of its English holdings other than Blyth – that is, the prior of Harmondsworth's lands and rights in Norfolk, Buckinghamshire and Sussex.[39] The long drawn-out process that followed has been well described elsewhere,[40] but, in short, a deal was struck at Rouen on 23 November 1390 and a price of 8,600 francs (£2,150) agreed:[41] the bishop, meanwhile, was to provide the prior of Harmondsworth, Robert Beauchamp and John le Cellier, 'son compaignon', with food, clothing, firing and any other things, for life, 'as it is fitting for religious [men] of such status to have'. Where they were to go is unclear – perhaps back to the abbey, to Blyth, to somewhere else in England, or they may simply have stayed on at the manor house.[42] Royal assent to the deal followed on 10 March 1391,[43] and on 25 October a receipt or acquittance for the same sum was received from the abbot.[44] The total cost of the transaction to Wykeham, including travel expenses, was £2,250.[45]

The Norfolk, Buckinghamshire and Sussex properties were added to the New College endowment,[46] but Winchester's Middlesex portfolio was enhanced with the nearby churches of Isleworth, Heston, Twickenham and Hampton (Fig 1), bought from the monks of Saint-Valery-sur-Somme (Somme).[47] As Harmondsworth was part of a number of properties including those in Norfolk, Sussex and Buckinghamshire,

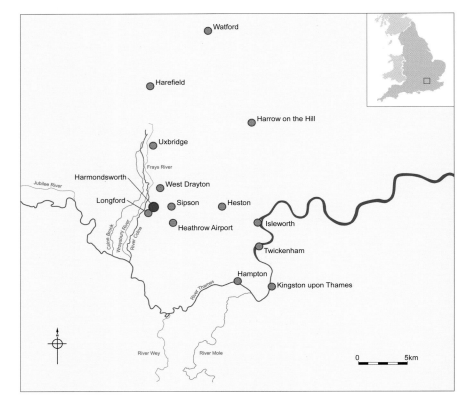

its own purchase price, and thus how good a bargain Wykeham had made, is
unknown.[48] The price paid for the package, however, would appear to have been as
much as 30 per cent above its value if calculated, as was commonly the case at the
time, as a multiple of 20 years' revenue;[49] or if (equally likely) the calculation was
based on the *taxatio* valuations of 1291 rather than real figures, at uncannily close
to the correct ratio.[50] Whatever the merits of the deal, however, Harmondsworth
became the second most valuable of Winchester's estates, yielding annual profits
in the period 1394–1410 exceeded only, in the same period, by those of Downton
(Wilts).[51]

The Harmondsworth property
Lands and resources

The college's acquisition was actually described only in the loosest terms in the
documents recording the transaction, for example, 'the manor of Harmondsworth
with appurtenances (including the advowson) and the abbot's other lands, tenements,
woods, rents, services and possessions in Harmondsworth, Ruislip and elsewhere
in Middlesex.'[52] No survey or extent (list and valuation of land and buildings) is
known to have been carried out for the new owners, nor is there a single surviving
terrier (description of land held by each tenant), which might have given the location
and extent of the manorial lands in some detail. Broadly speaking, however, the lands
of the manor were probably co-extensive with the parish, as recorded on Rocque's
map of 1754 (Fig 2), the Enclosure Allotment map of 1816 (Fig 3)[53] and again in
1860,[54] and which in 1951 covered 3,308 acres.[55] This is supported by the probable

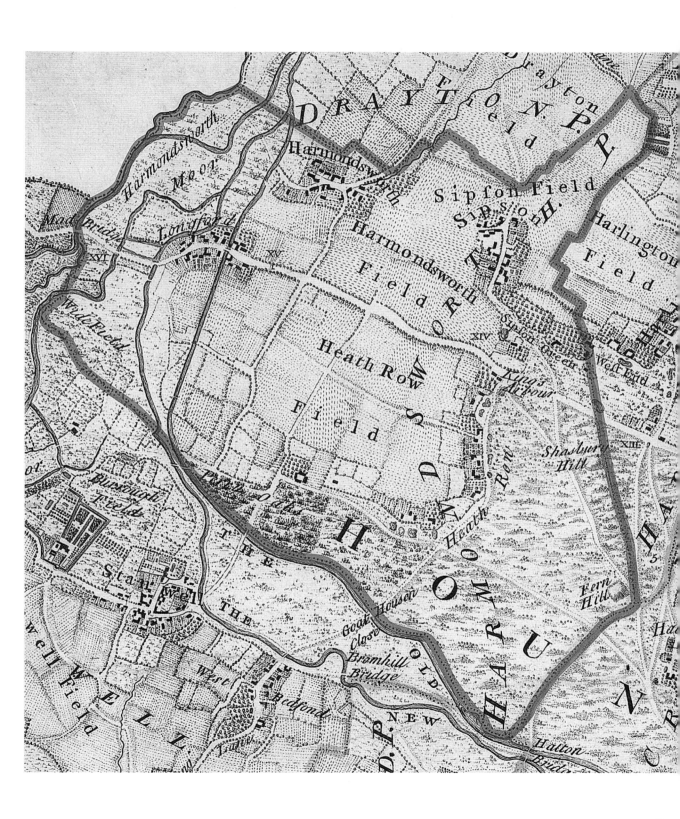

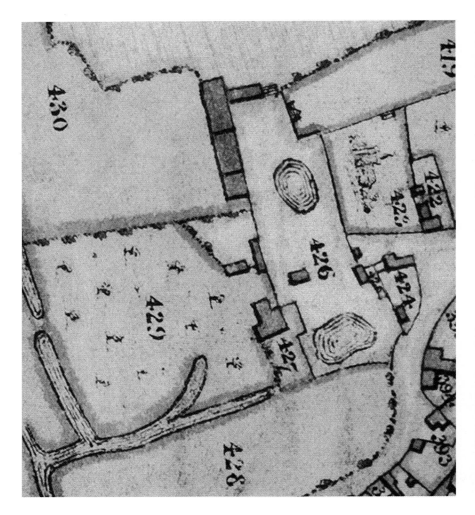

Fig 3
Section of the 1816
Harmondsworth Enclosure map,
showing the Great Barn and
associated buildings (north is to
the top). The barn (centre left)
is shaded in grey, the farmhouse
in red, and the church (top
left) sketched in in elevation.
Note the watercourses running
east–west to the south of the
farmyard and north–south to the
west. Transverse lines mark the
partitioning of the barn between
the three main tenants.
[Hillingdon Borough Archives,
Map 543]

pre-Conquest origins of the boundaries themselves, geographically circumscribing the parish but preceding its creation as an administrative unit.[56] Within its bounds lay the hamlets of Sipson, Longford and, in the Middle Ages, Southcote, perhaps replaced by the string of cottages facing Hounslow Heath marked on Rocque's map as 'Heath Row';[57] all but Sipson have since been swept away by the post-war expansions of the airport (initially established by the Fairey Aviation Company in 1930).[58] A series of rentals, meanwhile, allow the manor's arable acreage in and around the purchase period to be very roughly estimated. One dated to between 1370 and 1391, states that 'There are in this parish [sic] 38 virgators (customary tenants of about 30 acres), 39 semi-virgators and 45 cottars' (unfree tenants)[59] which, on the basis that a virgate was a measure of arable and usually 30 acres, and that a cottar's holding was of 5 acres, gives a total of 1,950. Similar figures are suggested by a rental of c 1350–91, giving minimum figures of (as for many entries no acreage is given) of 439¾ at Harmondsworth, 421½ at Sipson, 488 at Southcote and 438 at Longford, that is, a total recorded arable acreage of 1,787¼.[60] The manor is also likely to have had at least a small number of free tenants, not mentioned in the rental (either owing to error or accounted for elsewhere), whose holdings would have increased the total.[61] The rented acreage, by definition, also excluded the manorial demesne, within which the area down to cereals is known in at least eight years; in 1398, shortly after Wykeham's purchase, it stood at 201 acres, while the average, based on the eight years for which it is known between 1294 and 1451 was 236½ (see Table 1). On this basis, taking fallow into account,[62] another 470 acres or so could have been added to the total, although this would exclude substantial areas of non-arable demesne.

The medieval common field arrangement across which these acreages were scattered remains partly legible on Rocque's map, and suggests conformity to a particular west Middlesex arrangement whereby, rather than having two or three large fields of roughly equal size, a very large one was surrounded by a series of lesser neighbours: the crops were rotated between furlongs within the main field, and between the small fields in turn; examples included Ashford, East Bedfont, Feltham, Hanworth, West Drayton, Harlington and Hanworth.[63] Here, as marked by Rocque, 'Harmondsworth Field' is bordered by the smaller entities of 'Sipson Field', 'Heathrow Field', and 'Wide Field', while the more detailed Enclosure map of 1816 names 'Little Field', 'Bomer Field', 'Gravel Pit Field', 'Bury Mead', and 'Wide Mead' (the 'Wide Field' of 1754), although the age and origin of these secondary fields are unclear.[64] In 1461 a 'Southcote Field' is also mentioned.[65] At the edges of the arable to the south-east lay part of Hounslow Heath, and to the north-west, beyond (what was by 1754) an area of enclosed fields, Harmondsworth Moor;[66] on the eve of statutory Enclosure a total of 730 acres had already been enclosed.[67] Within the fields, both large and small, demesne and tenanted selions (strips of land) were intermixed in 'various furlongs', ie the major subdivisions of the open fields.[68] The names of the furlongs – if not necessarily all of them – appear in several documents: the rental of c 1377–91 lists under terra arabilis (arable land) the Merefurlong, Seffurlong, Suthstretfurlong, Weffurlong and the Middelfurlong, along with ten other named parcels, probably furlongs in all but name.[69] In the bailiff's account of 1406–7, the Southstretfurlong, Northstretefurlong and Woghfurlong appear again, the latter presumably being the Weffurlong of the earlier document.[70] Roughly where some of these furlongs lay can be guessed from names given on the 1816 map and 'pre-airport' six-inch Ordnance Survey maps – the meadow called Burymede in 1377–91, for example, presumably being the Bury Mead, just west of Longford, marked as parcel 482 in 1816, and the Holeway of 1406–7 being related to Holloway Lane, leading north out of Harmondsworth (today the A3044). The rental of c 1350–91 gives further topographical detail, grouping the tenants and their rents, in order, under 'Morelane', 'Shirlane', 'platea australis' (south street), 'Asshlane', 'Sebston waye', 'platea borealis' (north street), 'hamell de Subbeston', 'hammell de Southcote' and 'hammell de langforde'.[71] Some of these, clearly lanes or roads, can again be located from the maps of 1816 and later – 'Shirelane' as Cherry Lane, 'Asshlane' as Hatch Lane, and 'Sebston waye' as Sipson Road: more thorough attention might allow the medieval topography to be reconstructed in some detail. Other resources, as listed in an Extent of 1378 and other documents included two dovecotes, a garden, water mills for corn and malt, a fishery or fishpond – perhaps that mentioned in 1086 – customary works to the value of 14s, pannage and the revenues of the rectory at £13 6s 8d per annum.[72] The Domesday vineyard seems to have disappeared, in keeping with the general decline of English vineyards in the 14th century.[73]

In addition to the core at Harmondsworth, the abbey had retained and apparently augmented its property in Ruislip. This makes only fleeting appearances in the Harmondsworth documents, perhaps due to uncertainties as to its status: while the 13th-century custumal makes it clear that the 'abbot's tenants at Ruislip ... attend the court just as the men of Harmondsworth',[74] Ruislip is mentioned in the Extent of the manor in 1378 (value 20s) but not in those of 1293–4, 1324, 1337 or 1340, and at the time of Wykeham's purchase was a parcel of Harmondsworth but known as 'St Catherine's manor'.[75] Its chief value, however, seems to have been in pannage and timber: in 1086 Ruislip's major tenant, the abbey of Bec, had enough for 1,500 pigs (compared to Harmondsworth's 50); a *forestarius* (forester, forest manager) there in Holy Trinity's employ is mentioned in the custumal, its main value in 1547 being 'the woods called Westwoodde and Lowyshill',[76] and the manor remained heavily timbered into the 18th century.[77]

Buildings and early works at Harmondsworth

The buildings and premises inherited by the college at Harmondsworth are best understood from the records of repairs made to them in its early years as owner. Wykeham's policy was evidently to invest heavily and swiftly in the new foundation's estates, with both short- and long-term productivity in mind: between 1395 and 1402 new barns were built at Heston (Middlesex), Combe Bisset (Wilts), Hampton and Isleworth (Middlesex); others were repaired at Andwell (Hants) and Downton (Wilts); new chambers were added at Andwell (part surviving),[78] a new kitchen and hall at Farnham (Hants), a new hall at Durrington (Wilts), while the chambers, hall and chapel at St Cross (Isle of Wight) were repaired, and several mills were refurbished.[79] A new chancel was provided for the parish church at Hampton, another repaired at Twickenham, and the church at Hamble re-roofed.[80] Wykeham's programme made long-term sense, honoured the college's rectorial obligations and no doubt added to its prestige in the localities, but the warden and scholars were unimpressed: burdened with more immediate concerns, they petitioned him about the 'serious and intolerable expenses which we have yearly borne since the college's foundation in the building of churches, chapels, barns, houses and other works'.[81] No change of policy, however, seems to have ensued.

At Harmondsworth the first major initiative, between 1394 and 1397,[82] was the rebuilding of the chancel of St Mary's parish church. The work, or at least the window tracery, was done to the designs of the great master mason William Wynford (fl 1360–1403),[83] at a cost of about £68,[84] and survives largely as built.[85] Attention then turned to the former prior's house, mentioned, or mentioned in parts, in 1293–4, 1324, 1340, 1378, and 1381–2.[86] In or before 1395–1401, the college built a new chamber there,[87] and in 1398–9 work was done to adjoining walls and buildings.[88] As the account makes clear, and the 13th-century custumal and the inventories of 1324 and 1337 imply, the house consisted of the usual medieval components – hall, chamber, kitchen, pantry, buttery and latrine.[89] The timber-framed *tresaunce*, substantially repaired in 1388–9, was probably a covered way between two or more of them.[90] Why it was deemed necessary to maintain substantial houses at Harmondsworth and at other manors in the absence of a resident lord is explained by their regular if fleeting use by the college's officials, as places for manorial business (including the manorial court), and for cooking for and feeding large numbers of workers at particular times of year, notably during the harvest.[91]

Accompanying the house were the numerous other buildings of the manorial complex (*curia*), including two dovecotes mentioned in 1340[92] and 1378,[93] the 'lord's buildings' in 1387,[94] a cart-shed, dairy, cow-house, brew-house (1406–7),[95] a pighouse, stable, presshouse (possibly for wine, probably for cider) and a bakery (1388–9).[96] A granary (*granarium*) is mentioned on numerous occasions, including in the accounts for 1406–7, which note payments to two carpenters for 'felling the oak in the lord's garden and the trimming of the same for a stair to the granary door', suggesting that it was raised above the ground, or conceivably at first-floor level, as in the case of the surviving medieval granary at Bradford-on-Avon.[97] Outdoor areas mentioned include, in addition to the garden, noted in 1340 and 1378[98] (and as the 'lord's garden' 1406–7),[99] a rickyard (la ryckhawe) in 1388–9, and others, all walled, containing a dovecote (le culverhousehaugh), le dayehousehaugh (probably a dairy yard) and the bernhaugh (a barnyard, whatever it precisely meant).[100]

For as long as a complex of buildings had existed on this site and functioned as the domestic, administrative and operational centre of an agricultural and part-arable concern, it must have included a barn or barns for storing, at least, its demesne crops. In 1086, however, the first year for which any useful information exists, the demesne was probably smaller than in the 13th century and later, in keeping with the respective management practices of the time. This is suggested by the Domesday record of land for 20 ploughs, only 3 of which belonged to the demesne, making it just under one-sixth of the arable area, compared to the later medieval demesne of *c* 230 acres mentioned above, which covered nearer one-quarter of the total arable available.[101] As it happens, excavation at Harmondsworth in 1989 revealed the post-pits of a building measuring *c* 29m × 7.5m, to the north-east of and at roughly right-angles to the Great Barn, probably a barn, and perhaps dating from the years soon after 1069.[102] How long it lasted is unknown and too little is known about barns in England in the century or so that followed to speculate on the form of its earliest successors. By the mid- to late 12th century, however, the practice of perpetual institutions building large barns was clearly no novelty, as is shown (although none survive),[103] by the dimensions of that at Walton-on-the-Naze (Essex) at 51.20 × 16.15m (168ft by 53ft), built for St Paul's Cathedral and mentioned in a lease of 1142–68.[104] Standing examples in France, such as the abbey of Marmoutier's late 12th- or early 13th-century barn at Perrières (Calvados), or the recently destroyed timber building at Austrebosc (Eure, also probably Marmoutier's),[105] or the abbey of Ourscamp's magnificent stone-piered building of 1190–1 at Warnavillers (Oise),[106] tell the same story. Thus while it seems likely that, generally speaking, the practice of building very large demesne barns followed the late 12th-century return to demesne farming, prior to which great estates may more usually have received their tithes and payments in grain,[107] Harmondsworth may well have been equipped with an impressive structure or structures before 1200.

The first documented reference to a barn at Harmondsworth, however, beyond the general reference in Henry II's confirmation charter (1170–8) to the abbey's 'barns' in England,[108] is found in the 13th-century costumal. This shows that it (or they) was used for storing hay and sheaves of unspecified cereal or cereals (*bladum*), and for threshing. How many there were is not clear, but reference to the lord's barn (*grangia domini*) suggests deliberate distinction from a tithe barn, and so at least two.[109] The next two references to barns, both in 1324, remain ambiguous as to their number: the first, the account of the king's keepers (the estate being in the king's hands) Robert de Kelsey and Robert de Asschele, implies that the demesne crop of wheat, maslin (rye with wheat), barley, oats, beans and peas was being stored in a single barn,[110] but leaves it unclear as to whether tithe produce, not mentioned here, was stored in a second. The Extent of the same year, however, which valued the manor and the rectory separately, and might therefore have mentioned a tithe barn, fails to do so.[111] The next reference, in 1388–9, notes the 3d spent on 'the lathing of a certain panel of the wall of the barn', implying a timber-framed structure but nothing as to its function.[112] By 1397–8, however, there were certainly at least two barns at Harmondsworth and had been for some time, as is shown by the account of John Laner, bailiff, which itemises the costs of two carpenters hired for the mending of the beams of the porch of the wheat barn (*grangia frumenti*), the sill beam and the studding of two bays of the same barn at task 3s 4d. To 6,000 plain tiles bought for the same 37s 9d. To one-quarter of a bushel of stone lime bought for the same, 2s. To carriage of the same tiles and lime from Harefield to Harmondsworth by the lord's cart four times, 12d. To four bushels of oats bought for feeding the horses, 20d. To 700 laths bought for the same 3s 6d, both for lathing the said porch and for the small building (*domus*) next to the granary (*granarium*). To 6,500 lath nails bought for the same, 5s 10d at 14d per 1,000. To 250 hip tiles, valley tiles and ridge tiles (*hopetiell gotertiell et ryggetiell*) for the gutters, the said porch, the roof of the same and the roof of the aforesaid small house ... to the hire of one roofer roofing above the aforesaid porch ... together with various defects on the great barn (*magna grangia*) damaged by the great wind, at task, 26s 4d ... To one roofer hired to thatch with straw upon the great barn for 2 days, 12d.[113]

This shows that the 'wheat' barn was timber-framed, that it had at least one porch and, unless the hip-tiles were for the latter, probably hipped;[114] the 'stone lime' was presumably to repair a sill wall and/or for repairing 'torching' or rendering on the underside of replacement tiles.[115] Its condition, in particular the decay of major structural timbers, suggests it was of some age. Less is revealed about the other barn, but clearly it was thatched, and was presumably the bigger of the two. At its most literal meaning the word and form *frumenti*, ie 'of/for wheat', would imply its use for this alone, and the use of the other barn for other crops: such a distinction is reminiscent of the famous 'wheat' and 'barley' barns at Cressing Temple (Essex), an arrangement attested by numerous medieval sources[116] and found on big farms into modern times.[117] However, the situation at Harmondsworth is complicated by references to *three* barns under three other names in the accounts for 1406–7, two or all of which may have existed in 1390:[118] the terms of 1398 are here superseded by 'lord's' or 'demesne' barn (*grangia domini*), used for both hay and corn, the tithe barn (*grangia decime/arum*) and the 'hay barn' (*grangia feni*), which is mentioned for the first time;[119] the latter, incidentally, is likely to have been fully closed in, rather than open-sided, as in 1407 there is a mention of its door (*porta*).[120] Names, and possibly functions, may also have changed over time. Very probably, however, the 'great barn' (1397–8) and the 'demesne barn' (1406–7) were one and the same, the demesne yield being the larger, as would be expected and is implied by the smaller quantities of grain 'issued' from the tithe barn, for example, in 1406–7.[121] As a result it is tempting to conclude that the 'wheat barn' and the 'tithe barn' were synonymous, both being used for mixed crops, and that the 'hay barn' was a third structure of which little else is known.

Site layout before 1425–7

Something of the layout of the *curia* (court) into which the great barn was introduced can be worked out from documents dating both from before and after its construction. The best point of departure is the most securely located of the named structures, the medieval house, which stood to the south-west of the existing farm house of *c* 1820, about 200ft (61m) to the south of the great barn. This location relies on the identification of the house shown on the 1816 Enclosure map as the medieval house, more specifically the late medieval 'upper end' part not demolished in 1687 (*see* p 60). Its internal arrangement is unknown, but the accounts for 1397–8 show that the hall was aligned north–south.[122] The description of tiling work in the same account suggests that the 'lord's chamber' (*camera domini*) was associated with a 'little building' (*parva domus*) and that both were close to the granary, placing the latter near the house, as was the case with its successor of *c* 1820.[123] The garden probably lay nearby.[124] The reference in 1397–8 to roofing a (clay) wall 'extending from the small building near the granary to the great barn',[125] and that of 1406–7 to 'a wall extending from the corner of the great barn to the fence of the garden',[126] four perches and five feet long (71ft; 21.65m), hints at the proximity of the barn to the house and its garden. If – and this is an assumption, although supported by what can be deduced about the site layout from the 12th century[127] – the main axis of the complex as a whole was already north–south, the early 'great barn', identified above as the demesne barn, would have lain to the north of the house, garden and associated buildings, perhaps on the site of the existing barn. If so this would lend support to locating the second 'corn' or 'tithe barn' on the site apparently occupied by its successor of 1433–4, running east–west across the yard, 50ft (15.25m) to the south-east of the existing great barn.

Reference in 1440 to the 'gate of the curia' from which a path led to the door of the hall,[128] and post-medieval mentions of a 'gatehouse', presumably facing the village and principal access from the east,[129] suggests that the complex was surrounded by a secure perimeter, largely formed by the backs of its major buildings: other entrances probably existed in addition to the gatehouse, including a door (*porta*) next to the hay barn, repaired at a cost of 2d in 1406–7.[130] A number of authors have suggested that the complex was also moated,[131] based on the route of part-surviving watercourses or others known from the Enclosure map of 1816 (*see* Fig 3) and the Ordnance Survey map of 1894 (Fig 4). However, while Middlesex is rich in moated sites, here the watercourses surround a large area to the west of the barn and a total area of 7.75 acres, very different from the compact arrangement usually associated with 'homestead moats'[132] and other otherwise comparable sites such as New College's at Widdington (Essex).[133] Nor would the lie of land have made a circuit of standing water very practical,[134] and while respecting the layout of the site, certainly to the south, the main purpose of the watercourses was probably drainage rather than security.

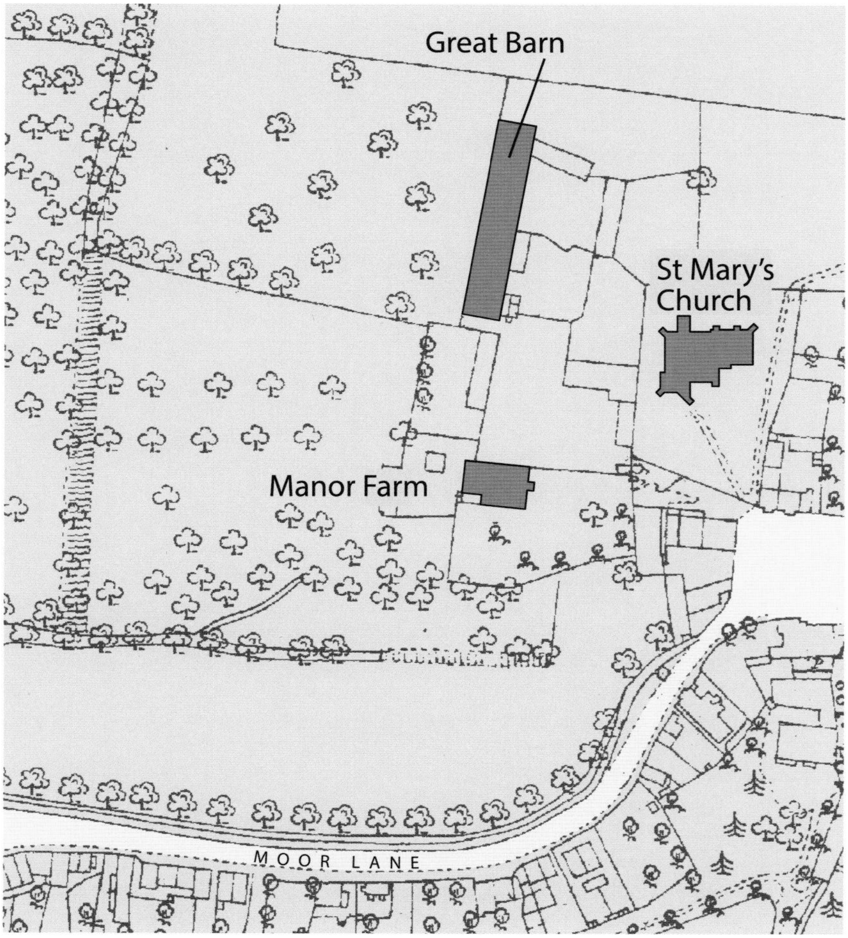

Fig 4
The OS 25in edition of 1894, showing the barn and its immediate environs (north at top). The barn, house and church are marked in red. The footprint of the barn is shown with various additions and lean-tos, removed in 1987. The priory house and its successors occupied a site just to the south-west of the farmhouse. [© Historic England Archive]

Building the Great Barn

Motivation and initiative

The need for a new barn arose, presumably, because the existing demesne barn was too small or beyond economic repair. Of these, capacity was perhaps the less important, as the total area put down to cereals seems to have varied very little since the late 13th century (Table 1), although the 42 per cent increase in the pulse crop (from 12.43 per cent to 18.40 per cent of the total) between 1293–4 and 1405–7, and bulkier in the ear, could have made this a factor: the latter increase itself probably owed, as elsewhere, to the extended use of peas to feed sheep.[135]

Table 1 shows the acreages of arable demesne put down to cereals and pulses in eight sample years in the period 1293–1451, during which the total area remained fairly constant. In the two years for which reaped and sown acreages are given, the crop reaped had been planted in the previous year (ie 1396–7 and 1449–50), and seed sown in winter and spring of 1397–8 and 1450–1.

Table 1 Acreages of arable demesne put down to cereals and pulses, 1293–1451

Year/s	Sown/reaped	Cereals	Pulses	Source
1293–4	sown	185	23	NA E101/2/1
1337 (22 July)	sown	200	33	NA C270/17 no. 7
1397–8	reaped	201	49	WCM 11502
1397–8	sown	212	39	WCM 11502
1406–7	sown	192	41	WCM 11503
1433–4	reaped	205	40	NA SC6/1126/7
1450–1	reaped	193	40	WCM 11504
1450–1	sown	236.5 acres		WCM 11504
Average (both crops)		**236.18**		

On the issue of condition, we know only that the 'corn barn' and the 'great barn' had been repaired in 1388–9, and can imagine that, 35 years on, at least one of the buildings could have decayed beyond economic repair. Rebuilding may also have been prompted, if more than 20 years after his death, by a continuation of Wykeham's own systematic policy of improving the infrastructure at his major estates. Not inconsistent with this, the initiative may have been further encouraged, justified and made affordable by the manor's recent economic success and expectations for its future. This is illustrated by the receipts for the seven years between and including 1394–5 to 1400–1, averaging £50 12s 7d, compared to those of 1417–18 to 1425–6 (excepting 1418–19), at £70 12s 5d, respectively:[136] although there were major annual fluctuations, such as in the bumper year of 1396–7 at £101 14s ½d and the poor one of 1424–5 at £45 16s 8d,[137] the increase must have been noticeable.

The personality and initiative of the bailiff Roger Hubbard, for whom a new building would have had obvious advantages, may also have played a part, as it did for example at Enstone (Oxon) where, according to an inscription, Winchcombe Abbey's barn was built in 1382 'at the entreaty of Robert Mason, bailiff of this place'.[138] Although little is known of Hubbard, he was in office from early 1421–2 to 1447–8,[139] and although he ran into difficulties later on, was clearly in favour with the college in 1425.[140] Warden Thurbern, in office 1413–50, although a willing enough builder in Winchester, is not known to have had any part in the initiative.[141]

Size and specification

The decision to build the Great Barn was accompanied by others as to its size, materials, general form, appearance and permissible cost. On the issue of size, the most obvious determinant, it might be expected, would have been the approximate volume required to store the crop from an approximate acreage, or its upper limit, present or predicted. To what extent was this the case at Harmondsworth? As we know the volume of the barn, and have a sound idea of the acreages down to cereal and pulses between the late 13th and the mid-15th century (*see* Table 1), this is at least worth exploring. The perils, though, of such calculations are obvious: the numerous variables and unknowns, including the useable volume as envisaged by the builders, the size of the acres in question, yield per acre, how much and how often part of the cereal and pulse crop was stored in ricks,[142] in sheaf size and variations in stacking methods, and how much hay the barn housed, make only 'order-of-magnitude'-type figures attainable.

The total interior volume of the Harmondsworth building, carefully calculated, adds up to 4,953m³,[143] but if the entrance bays were left empty to allow for access and threshing, as is probable,[144] the useable volume would have amounted to 3,706m³. Medieval sources show, not surprisingly, that barns, and different parts of them, could be filled to different extents, particularly with respect to use of the roof space: to below eaves level (*sub severundas*),[145] to wall-plate level (*in altum equale murum*),[146] to tiebeam level (*ad trabeam*),[147] to 'above the height of the walls' (*excedentes altitudinem murorum*),[148] to collar-beam level (*ad trabem furcarum*)[149] and to the ridge (*ad festum*).[150] Filling to tiebeam level, however, may have been a more usual arrangement,[151] and above the collar, where present, discouraged by the difficulty of handling sheaves in a confined, hot, dark, dusty and obstructed space. At Harmondsworth, the volume available for such use, that is, up to the upper surfaces of the nave tiebeams, would have been 3,310m³.

The correlation between volume and the acreage it would have taken to fill the barn can be sought in two ways: first, using medieval sources for the quantities of grain which could be stored, in the ear, in a given volume, and matching the useable volume of the barn with the acreage required to produce it; second, taking the estimated volume of sheaves produced by the estimated acreage and comparing it to the known useable volume of the barn. The evidence for the first approach comes from two sources, one being a 15th-century annotation to a text of 14th-century origin from St Peter's Abbey, Gloucester, known as the 'Gloucester Husbandry'.[152] This states that wheat-sheaves stacked in a barn 30ft wide, within a bay of 15ft and to a wall-height of 10ft, ie with a volume of 4,500ft³ (or 126m³), 'will commonly contain 40 quarters',[153] giving an in-sheaf volume per quarter of 112ft 6in³ (3.15m³). The second resides in the grain content of two stacks belonging to Worcester Cathedral Priory between 1400 and 1430, giving in-sheaf volumes per quarter of 4.87m³ and 3.58m³, averaging at 4.22m³.[154] Dividing the useable volume of the Harmondsworth barn (3,310m³) by the 'Gloucester' volume would give an in-ear capacity for 1,050 quarters. Assuming that, by the accepted norm, each acre of land produces 1.3 quarters, it would then have taken 807 acres to fill it; applying the same calculation to the 'Worcester' volume of an in-sheaf quarter at 4.87m³, it would have taken 522 acres of wheat to fill the barn, and at 3.58m³, 522 acres, and at the average (4.22m³), 603 acres. Given that the average demesne area down to cereals in the known years in and between 1293–4 and 1450–1 is 198 acres, by these calculations the crop would have filled the barn to between 25 per cent and 50 per cent capacity.

The alternative approach, starting with land area and the estimated bulk of the crop, clearly requires an estimate of the number of sheaves produced per acre and of their individual volume. Taking John Weller's estimate that an acre of land produced 80 sheaves, and that a compressed sheaf occupied 0.056m³,[155] Harmondsworth's 198 acres would have produced 15,840 sheaves, taking up 887m³ of space – again, far less than the building provided. Their figures are, however, open to question: most importantly, practical experience suggests that Weller's sheaf-per-acre estimate is too low: Stephen Letch, longstanding grower of (drilled) long-straw wheat in Norfolk, advises that, with minimal fertiliser input, between 400 and 500 sheaves per acre represents a normal yield; other growers, using more fertiliser, claim up to 700.[156] On the other hand, Letch estimates the volume of a compressed sheaf at the lower figure of 0.025m³, which also accords better with some medieval evidence, including advice in a 13th-century farming treatise,[157] and medieval depictions such as the famous threshing scene in the Luttrell Psalter (see Fig 21). But if this lower figure is used, even if multiplied by 400 (his lowest sheaf per acre yield) and again by 198, the resulting total sheaf volume is 1,980m³; if the 500 figure is used, the result is 2,475m³. Even at the higher estimate, and assuming that demesne tithes were stored with the rest of the demesne crop, the comfortably useable volume of the barn would have been no more than 74 per cent occupied by cereals.

The disparity between the results of the two approaches raises questions about the value of both, but preference should probably, if perhaps unhelpfully, be given to the first (even though the 'Gloucester' and 'Worcester' figures differ), for they at least rely on three measurements (land area, related crop volume and storage space) based on medieval evidence. But how then do we explain the gap between barn and crop volumes? The possibility that the college was planning for a vast expansion of the estate is impossible, if only thanks to the statutes of Mortmain, while a radical change of land use can be discounted largely on practical grounds. Meanwhile, Brady's suggestion that the disparity ('almost two and half times larger than was needed to store the crops from the entire manor'),[158] owed, as he suggests also of other buildings, to the 'prestige' value of an over-large building, is neither easy to reconcile with Winchester's wholly business-like approach to such matters nor likely to have succeeded. Nor is a 'gross' disparity on this scale due to miscalculation. The answer probably lies, then, either in the extent (particularly the height) to which filling the interior was envisaged, or what was stored there in addition to cereals. The first variable is hard to address, but it is worth noting, because if the barn was filled to, say, a metre below tiebeam height, then the useable volume would have been reduced to about 2,736m³. On the issue of other crops, we know for example that in 1433–4, 48 quarters and 6 bushels of pulse were recorded 'of the issue of both barns' (de exitu ambarum grangie),[159] ie of the demesne barn and tithe barn. Here the 'Worcester' figures are once again of interest, as they show that in one instance a quarter of peas in sheaf occupied 8.28m³ and in another 13.8, thanks to the bulk of leaf and stalk compared to the peas and beans themselves. On this basis the volume occupied by the pulse crop in both barns in 1433–4 would have been either c 669m³ or 400m³, and if the higher figure is added to a cereal volume of 2,475 (above), this would have taken the occupied capacity up to a maximum of 3,148m³, ie 98.86 per cent.

Finally, we need to add hay: there was a hay barn at Harmondsworth (*see* p 10), which must have taken some or even most of the crop, roughly quantifiable on the basis of the requirement of customary tenants to cut, carry and pitch it. But these added up to hundreds of cartloads – 308, for example, in 1406–7, and as much as 496 in 1433–4, and even if a small (if no doubt annually variable) quantity of this was stored in the great barn, in addition to grain and pulses, it could have been filled to capacity.[160] If so, it can be argued that its size was indeed designed with the average mixed produce of the demesne in mind. This is in keeping with similar conclusions drawn about other buildings: in particular, Charles Higounet's that the abbey of Châalis's giant barn at Vaulerent (Seine-et-Oise), was, with a capacity of 6,000–7,000m³, carefully specified to store the produce of the 380-hectare (939 acres) demesne, worked according to a variant of the three-field system.[161]

Scale apart, there were of course specification issues to do with materials and design, and the college's decisions in this respect are easily explained. First, the decision to build all but the sill walls in timber made good sense in the absence of any good local building stone and the much lower cost, per cubic foot of interior space provided, that timber-framing allowed (Fig 5). Second, the choice of design of the building was, unsurprisingly, based on the tried and tested format of a broad central nave and aisles, although there are peculiarities in its

Fig 5
The Great Barn from the south-west. The building looks much as it must have done in the 15th century, when the vast expanse of roof was covered, as now, in clay tiles, although the eaves then descended slightly lower. The vertical boarding to the side walls is largely original, although blackened by repeated coatings of tar since the early 19th century. [N120001 © Historic England Archive]

detailing (*see* pp 26–29). Unusual care was taken, however, to use large, straight, well-dressed timbers, resulting not only in an exceptionally durable structure, but an appearance of dignity, solidity and regularity not apparent in all great barns, although we can only speculate as to whether this was the college's deliberate intention.

Cost

Exactly how much the building cost is unknown, but a few specific expenses are recorded and others can be roughly estimated, allowing an 'order of magnitude' figure to be suggested. Itemised costs are confined to the 8d paid to John atte Oke in 1424–5,[162] and the £2 7s 6d paid for nails and ironwork, the £6 released to the bailiff 'in costs for the same barn',[163] the £1 given as bonus to Roger Helyer, tiler, and the 12s 9d's worth of expenses claimed on behalf of the warden and John Edmond paid out in 1426–7,[164] adding up to £10 0s 3d.

Rough estimates for other specific costs can be made by multiplying the unit costs for materials given elsewhere in the Winchester accounts by those needed, as deduced from today's requirements or the fabric and dimensions of the building. By this means, for example, it can be estimated that the roof tiles cost £16 10s, laths £2 5s 6d, lath nails £2 1s, board nails 16s 6d and boards £4 0s 1d. Labour costs can be estimated, very roughly, in the case of battening and tiling, by multiplying the 320 man days recently expended on this very task in 2013[165] by the 15th-century tilers' day-rate of 4d,[166] producing a figure of £5 6s 8d.

The expenditure of much more substantial sums, however, is implied by the counter roll and bursars' accounts, respectively, for the years 1425–6 and 1426–7.[167] The first records an annual profit of £87 6s 8d, but notes that £29 6s 8d's worth of this was 'cancelled on the bursars' roll', and so not received centrally, for which the obvious and best explanation is that it was spent, at source, on the barn.[168] Given the stages of construction suggested below (pp 29–33), this may have been spent on building the sill wall and felling, transporting and stockpiling the main structural timbers. The bursars' account for the following year (1426–7), however, notes under Harmondsworth that 'from Roger Houbard, bailiff, nothing this year because all to building the new barn there',[169] implying that the costs of the barn had consumed the manor's entire profit for that year. The sum itself is unrecorded, but the equivalent figure for 1424–5 had been £45 16s 8d, for 1428–9 £54 3s 10d (and on average between 1394–5 and 1492–3, £67 5s 2d)[170] suggesting an expenditure in that year from the manorial receipts, of at least £50. This, the more substantial sum, was probably spent on the conversion of the stockpiled timber and prefabricating the main elements of the structural frame, the relatively fiddly and expensive costs of boarding, framing doors and other details, and the roofing (for which extrapolated costs have been suggested above). This sum was not, however, quite enough, as in the last year £6 was also required from the college's central coffers.[171]

Avoiding double counting by omitting extrapolated costs, the known figures, together with the estimated spend of £50 in 1426–7, add up to £87 7s 7d. To these should be added, perhaps, the cost of the timber and its felling and carriage: an idea of the possible cost may be given by the £41 6s 5d (49 per cent) of a total cost of £83 8s ½d) incurred under these headings in building the smaller barn (dimensions unknown, but covered with 65,000 tiles as opposed to Harmondsworth's 80,000) for the Bishop of Winchester at Ivinghoe (Bucks) in 1309–10, although the figure may reflect the manor's atypical remoteness from other diocesan properties from which materials could have been drawn;[172] at Harmondsworth the college may have avoided much of the purchase cost (£33 1s 3d at Ivinghoe) by drawing materials from its own (or perhaps diocesan) property in the vicinity, such as the former's at Isleworth, Heston, Hampton or Ruislip. If so, we can expect a cost more akin to that for stone, timber and carriage in building Glastonbury's barn of 1340–3 at Street (Somerset), measuring 39 × 8.9m, sited amid a dense concentration of the abbey's properties, at only £9 4s 7d, or 17 per cent of the total.[173]

As a measure of its value, the figure of just over £87 can be compared to expenditure in 1401 on a new barn and a new granary at Isleworth, and a new barn at Hampton, built at a total cost of £146 8s 9d (partly met by £57 6s 6d supplied by the treasurer of Wolvesey Palace, ie the bishop's exchequer);[174] both barns, intended for rectorial use only (ie for tithes and glebe produce) must have been substantially smaller than the Great Barn. This would independently suggest, in 'order of magnitude' terms, that a sum between approximately £50 and £100 would have built the Great Barn. The figure also makes sense in comparison to sums paid for other barns in the 14th and 15th centuries. Particularly useful are the accounts of 1358–9 for the building of Merton College's new barn at Gamlinghay (Cambs):[175] this was a five-bay structure, wholly timber-framed, with daubed walls, two main doors (probably opposed), and measuring roughly 36.5 × 13.6m, that is, with a floor area of about 493m²: as such it was 176m² smaller than Harmondsworth, although differently proportioned, and requiring, at nearly 80,000, a similar number of tiles to roof it. The total cost of the Gamlinghay barn was about £40: about £8 per bay, or about 19½d per square metre, unit costs which if applied to Harmondsworth (although not allowing for the inflation in wage and material prices between the 1350s and the 1420s),[176] produce figures of £96 and £54, within the suggested cost range of the Middlesex building.[177]

The Gamlinghay accounts also provide interesting itemised costs unknown at Harmondsworth, such as the 10s for groundworks, and the expense, perhaps surprisingly small, 'of the carpenter and men … [for] raising the great timbers for the new barn … 3s 10d' (ie, the process, in the case of Harmondsworth, illustrated by Fig 18). The Ivinghoe account offers similar information, including the actual carpenters' work to the (wholly timber-framed) building at £14 6s 8d, and 19d and food for hiring extra men to erect the trusses.[178]

Incidentally, the costs of these enormous but wholly or largely timber-framed buildings compare interestingly to those (their roofs apart) of stone: New College, for example, spent at least £123 on its new barn at Swalcliffe (Oxon) a smaller building (39 × 6.9m internally), but with 4.8m-high stone walls, in the period 1400–1 to 1406–7;[179] if ornament was involved, the cost increased exponentially, as shown by the £68 Winchester paid out to rebuild the diminutive chancel of Harmondsworth church in 1394–7.[180]

Not least, in comparison with those for its more lavish creations, the strictly 'business case' for the college's investment was undoubtedly sound. Calculating the return on investment derived from the specific contribution of the barn to manorial income and profit per year would be impossible or uselessly imprecise, but is unlikely to have been a consideration at the time: a barn was necessary, come what may, and under whatever land management regime prevailed, for the manorial economy to function and profit to be made. As it was, the capital would have been paid back by between one and two years' profit from the manor, and while less could have been spent, in the centuries since, the Great Barn's solid construction has kept 'depreciation' and maintenance to a minimum – if, as it happened, largely for the benefit of owners other than the college.

Personnel

References in the Harmondsworth documents to the barn's construction and the people involved are few but informative. First, the Winchester bursars' account for 1424–5 records payment, mentioned above, of 8s to '*Johanni atte Oke iuxta Kyngston ad videndum meremium cum Willelmo Kyppyng pro grangia de Hermondesworth*' (John atte Oke near Kingston for viewing timber with William Kyppyng for the barn of Harmondsworth). John is not known with certainty from any other source: atte Oke was a common name in the Middle Ages and could denote either an individual from or living at Oke, or have been an inherited second name: the preferred reading of *iuxta Kyngston* (ie by or near Kingston (on Thames), although not that of John Harvey,[181] is that it described Oke's current habitation, in which case the source of the timber is unknown.

Who designed the barn is not clear. Features and idiosyncrasies of the structure itself suggest no more than someone who had worked in the area to the west of London, Buckinghamshire and Oxfordshire. Of Kyppyng, described later in the same text as *carpentarius*, little is known, other than that in 1423–4 he was paid £6 for works to the chancel at Downton (Wilts), and that, according to Harvey, he was 'probably the "William Carpenter" paid 6s 8d in the same year for work at Andover', and in 1424–5 'for seats in the entry of the college chapel, at a rate of 1s 4d a week (2½d per day) for himself and 1s 3d for his two servants'.[182] At Downton, where the liturgical chancel comprised both choir and transepts (all east of the screen), the existing low-pitch south transept roof may well be his work; the Winchester work does not survive.[183] The carpenter John Kypyng [sic], who worked on the college's house at Andwell (Hants) in the early 1390s was perhaps his father or other relative.[184] William's role in building the barn at Harmondsworth is unclear, but his rate of pay in 1424–5, at less than half the 6s 8d daily pay awarded to 'ordinary well-qualified carpenters', let alone the 1s per day commanded by carpenters of 'national repute', might normally suggest that design and supervision were in other hands.[185] Conversely, however, the mistakes and oddities of the barn's construction might suggest that Kyppyng was indeed in charge – perhaps newly promoted, or hired on the cheap, or in the absence of a better candidate. Possible alternatives, however, may be suggested, notably John Wyltsher and John Gylkes, working at New College in or very close to those years,[186] and of whom the second may have designed the (albeit very different) roof at Swalcliffe.[187] William Wyse, who had worked on the roofs of the churches at Heston, Isleworth and Harmondsworth,[188] is a possibility too, but is last heard of in 1415.[189] A Thomas Waso, conceivably a relative of Wyse's, also mentioned in the 1424–5 account and handsomely rewarded for his work at Alresford (Hants), may be another.

Other people involved in the barn's construction are named in the bursars' accounts for 1426–7: 12s 9d in expenses and gifts covered the travel costs of warden Thurburn and John Edmond in visiting Robert Keton (the London-based chancellor of the diocese of Winchester 1399–1429)[190] and en route, on 3 August 'for the viewing of the carpenters and tilers working on the barn newly built at Harmondsworth in the month of August'.[191] The same account names John Derfford, smith, and Roger Helyer, tiler, who received 20s 'over and above the contracted price for the roofing of the said barn', presumably as a bonus for a job well done.[192]

Date

Whatever uncertainties may surround the cost of the barn and the people involved, there can be little doubt as to when the practical work of its construction was begun or completed. The bursars' accounts tell us not only that the timber was 'viewed' in 1424–5, but that by September 1427 money had been spent on carpenters' and tilers' materials and John Edmond's expenses for viewing 'the barn newly built at Harmondesworth' (*de novo aedificata*), ie on a building which was substantially complete:[193] the implication, clearly, is that the barn was built between September 1424 and September 1427. Confirmation and finessing of this, however, and proof that it was *this* barn to which the accounts refer, comes from the all-important and recently amplified dendrochronological evidence. The first useful sampling and analysis was carried out by Ian Tyers in 1990, on six offcuts taken from an arcade plate during McCurdy's repairs, which produced a single precise felling date (sample 4) of spring 1426.[194] In 2012 further precision and information on the building's phasing was sought by taking another 14 samples. The process was hampered by the friability of the sapwood, but produced another felling date, of winter 1424/5, from a sill beam (sample 17) and a series of approximate felling dates ranging from *c* 1423 to *c* 1426. All the other sampled timbers, nevertheless, produced dates consistent with the felling dates of winter 1424/5 and spring 1426.[195] The combined evidence shows, therefore, that felling for the barn began in the winter 1424–5 (consistent with Kyppyng having identified the standing timber in the autumn of 1424) and continued, or was resumed, in the spring of 1426. Theoretically, construction could have begun early as the first months of 1425, green timber being felled and supplied as needed (green timber being preferred to seasoned timber thanks to its ease of working). For practical reasons, however, all the timber for the principal frame would probably have been required before its prefabrication began, while the felling date of *c* 1426 attributed to an arcade post (sample 7), and of *c* 1425 to a mid-rail (sample 8) strongly suggest that the framing was not begun before 1426.[196] On balance, therefore, it seems most likely that the frame was prefabricated during 1426 and erected during the spring and summer months of 1427. The sill wall, meanwhile, could have been built at any time from 1424 to the summer of 1426, assuming that the work was carried out at the most suitable season and was allowed to dry out and settle before taking the weight of the frame.

Description, structural history and significance

Masonry components and flooring

The barn's sill walls are of some structural interest in themselves and in relation to the building and phasing of the whole (*see* Figs 16 and 17). These were built on a broader trench-built foundation, in many places now exposed by the erosion of the ground outside, and rise (in total) up to 1.6m above existing ground level (south-east corner) and as little as 0.5cm (north-west).[197] Although near-perfectly rectangular in plan (Fig 6), the walls are astonishingly poorly levelled, the west wall dropping almost 0.3m (12 inches) from north to south, and the east wall as much as 0.13m (5 inches). These imperfections were not corrected by

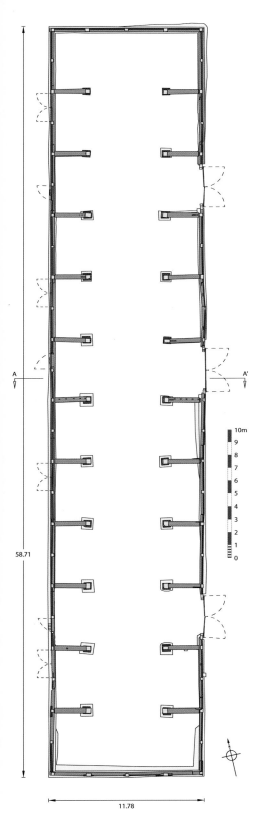

levelling the sill beams, and so had an important effect on the form of the timber superstructure as a whole.

The fabric is largely of roughly shaped blocks (up to 1.1m long) of ferricrete (Fig 7), an iron-oxide cemented river gravel, hard to dress but which can be cut more easily when newly quarried. This is of local origin (although not from the site of the barn itself), and was used as a major

Fig 6 (left)
Plan of Harmondsworth Great Barn.
[Based on Kohnert 2012, 4
© Historic England Archive]

Fig 7 (above)
Detail of the sill wall showing the blocks of 'ferricrete', a local iron-rich conglomerate, and the sparing use of Reigate stone. Note the horizontal ledge or offset marking the break between the trench-built foundation and the wall proper. As elsewhere in the building, several phases of post-medieval repair can be identified.
[Courtesy Dr Tillman Kohnert]

Fig 8 (right)
Hexafoil or 'Daisy wheel', probably an apotropaic mark, inscribed on the Reigate stylobate at truss 10, adjacent to the northernmost door.
[Courtesy Dr Tillman Kohnert]

building material in the 14th century at the church of St Peter and St Paul at Harlington and St Mary's, Harrow on the Hill.[198] Small fragments are also incorporated in the tower (*c* 1500), the late 12th-century south aisle and the chancel (1394–7) of St Mary's Harmondsworth.[199] Its use in the barn, however, is one of the latest as a primary building material and the blocks among the largest known.[200] Between the ferricrete blocks are a number of levelling courses of clay peg-tiles, others of which were used to level up the masonry under the timber sills. On the south and east sides and part of the west the gaps in the ferricrete facing are filled with roughly trimmed flint nodules, also of local extraction, and occasional pieces of Reigate stone;[201] the north part of the west wall and the north wall are less carefully built, probably because they faced the exterior of the manorial complex and not the main approach. All four (external) corners and the door openings were originally quoined in Reigate ashlar, now mostly replaced.

Internally, the arcade posts rest on single blocks of Reigate stone averaging about 0.75 × 0.55 × 0.55m.[202] The Reigate blocks are inscribed with a wide variety of symbols, some probably masons' marks, and some resembling carpenters' plumb and level marks, although their purpose here is unclear. The incised multifoils, probably dating from *c* 1750–1850, and probably apotropaic marks, are described below (p 60) (Fig 8).[203]

The original flooring was simply the natural brick-earth sub-soil, as has been demonstrated archaeologically, and which remains exposed today at the north end.[204] Whether the flooring in the three entrance bays was originally treated differently, for example with boarding or flagstones, is unclear. Hartshorne's view of 1873 clearly shows two boarded floors, labelled as 'threshing floors' on his plan, in all three entrance bays,[205] of which the surviving boarding in the third (southernmost) entrance bay is presumably a survival, but is of deal and probably 19th-century. Whether these were actually threshing floors, or simply hard-standing in the streys for other practical purposes, let alone whether this was the arrangement in the 15th century, is unclear: medieval threshing floors identified elsewhere, such as at Swalcliffe in Oxfordshire[206] could be paved or simply made of earth, and were no doubt sometimes boarded, as they often were in the post-medieval period.[207] The 'wood threshing floor … formed of thick oak, black with age and polished by the beating of flails for many generations till it had grown as slippery and as rich in hue as the state-room floors of an Elizabethan mansion'[208] in the 'great barn' at Weatherbury, described by Thomas Hardy in *Far from the Madding Crowd* , would perhaps have been as familiar a sight in the 15th century as it was in the 19th. But on the whole, what we know about medieval threshing floors appears to be very limited; no documentary references are known to the present authors, other, perhaps, than to an *area* built in a barn of Norwich Cathedral Priory at Hindringham (Norfolk) in the late 13th century.[209] Meanwhile the archaeological and structural evidence for floors laid for threshing (if in addition to other reasons), or at least their identification, seems to be equally poorly understood.[210]

The timber framing[211]

The main structure consists of large square-sectioned arcade posts with thickened jowled heads jointed to both arcade plate and tiebeam. The arcade posts are braced to the tiebeams by large slightly concave braces, with similar braces to the arcade plates (Figs 9 and 10).

The main roof is of simple principal rafter with collar and crown-strut form with butt purlins and windbraces, but no ridge piece. The half-hipped ends of the roof are supported by an arch-braced intermediate principal rafter collar truss that receives

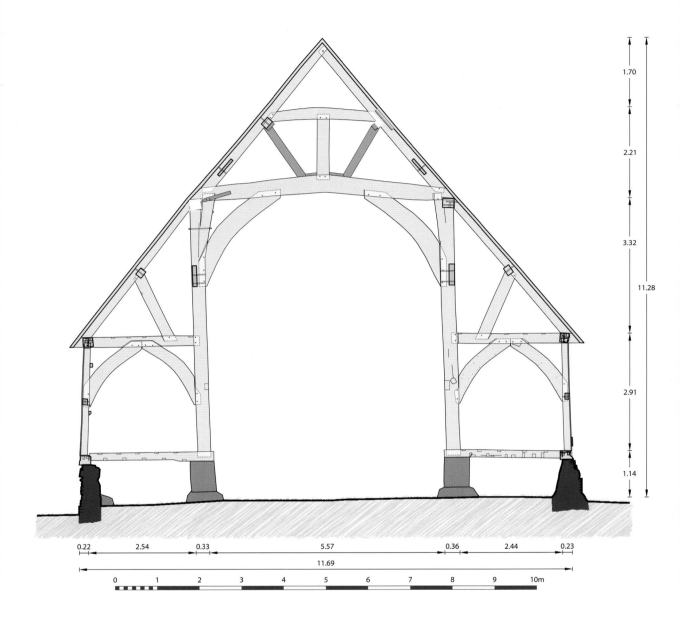

Fig 9
North face of Truss 7.
[Based on Kohnert 2012, 4
© Historic England Archive]

the end of the purlins and supports the hip rafters in mid-span. There is a small gablet above each hip (Fig 11). The rafters themselves are largely original.

The aisles have aisle ties that interrupt the aisle wall plates and have a raking strut that engages with the principal rafter and clasps a single purlin for the aisle. The aisle trusses are braced by a pair of braces meeting under the aisle ties, and each truss has a sill beam that engages with the aisle walls at one end and supports the arcade plates at the other. The wall framing to the aisles consists of a centre stud and middle rail, resting on the sill beam. Interestingly, there are no braces in the side walls, the barn relying for longitudinal bracing – evidently successfully – entirely on the arcade

Fig 10 (right)
Isometric drawing of the assembly at the head of the aisle posts and, to the right, exploded to illustrate construction. The vertical timber is the aisle post, and the large horizontal timber, propped by a curved brace and projecting to the left, is the tie beam extending over the nave of the barn. The arrangement here is of a type common in English carpentry from the 14th to the 17th century. Elsewhere the carpentry includes some more unusual features.
[Based on Kohnert 2012, 11
© Historic England Archive]

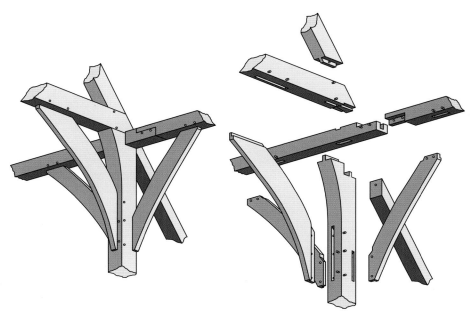

Fig 11 (below)
Photograph showing the construction of the half hip and gablet at the north end of the barn. Note the subsidiary truss standing on the arcade plate, propping the common rafters to the hip, an ingenious arrange-ment illustrating the skill of the carpenter.
[Courtesy Dr Tillman Kohnert]

braces. The ends of the barn similarly have a centre post, a heavy middle rail set just above the aisle ties with subsidiary rails above and below.

The scantling of the timber is generally substantial if not massive, with the arcade posts ranging from 12in to 18in square (0.35–0.46m²) at the base, and widening to as wide as 27in (0.69m) at the top of the jowl. Arcade plates are 9in high by 10–11in wide (0.23 × 0.25.5–0.28m), and the tiebeams are of a similar width to the arcade posts and up to 19in (0.48m) high. Arcade braces and transverse braces extend down the arcade posts to similar levels and vary between 4in and 6in thick (0.1–0.15m) and 10in to 14in wide (0.25–0.35m) in the case of the arcade braces and 12in to 19in (0.3–0.48m) in that of the main transverse braces. The principals are slightly tapering, and are slightly thicker than the collars and crown struts.

While there is obvious pairing of sawn timbers in each truss and arcade bay, no effort was made to achieve real consistency between trusses in the shape and section of braces or scantling of tiebeams. Some tiebeams and collars are cambered, even slightly cranked (T4, T11 and T12), while others are more irregular, resulting from the natural form of the trees (T5).

Thanks to the even number of bays, the three doors are asymmetrically placed, the central door being just off centre, in bay 7, with the other doors in the third bay from each end (bays 3 and 10) (see Fig 6). The door posts all have distinctive jowled heads and are connected to the timber frame by the extended ends of the sills and a short middle rail. The tops of the posts are tenoned into the wall plate with two pegs.

The timber walls of the barn were clad from the outset, as has now been confirmed by dendrochronology,[212] with vertical sawn oak boards, up to 0.45m wide and approximately 25mm thick. Those on the end elevations and the south end of the west side have been replaced, but on the other elevations they largely survive, and their upper parts, where protected by the eaves, are in near-pristine condition. The wall plates and sill beams are neatly rebated for the boards, and the mid-rail set in from the face of the posts by a corresponding depth, allowing the boards to lie flush with the sill beam, wall plate and central stud. The boards were nailed in place at top and bottom and butt-jointed edge to edge, although in many places battens have since been nailed over the joints.

As originally built, as observed by Drury,[213] the eaves projected further than today, the lowest one or two courses of tiles being fixed to taper-section boards, perpendicular to the rafters, and extending beyond the rafter feet. This was a common medieval arrangement,[214] but is indicated at Harmondsworth by the clear difference in the condition of the upper surfaces of the rafter-feet at their lower extremities, where protected by the boards, and the area above, less well protected by the tiles alone.[215] The hatches on the west side of the barn – not original but pre-dating the truncation of the eaves – show the maximum extent to which the latter could have projected, while allowing the hatches to open, to have been about 0.4m. The fact that the ends of the rafter feet were originally cut horizontally (ie on the same plane as the ground, rather than at right-angles to the main axis of the rafter) so as to give a clean, uninterrupted eaves line, is perhaps an indication of the designer's sensibility to aesthetic effect.

The barn retains a good and fairly complete set of assembly marks (Fig 12). Each truss is numbered I to XIII from south to north, with a tag (an extra incised stroke) being used on the east side to differentiate between east and west. There seems to have been a little confusion in the numbering and the use of tags on the west side of trusses 4, 5, 8, and the east side of truss 9. In addition, there is an abundance of plumb and level marks, mostly on smoothed sections of the hewn timbers, and mostly found two or three feet below the arcade plate on the arcade posts. Most of the plumb and level marks consist of three lines across the face of the timber with a pair of

Fig 12
Assembly marks.
[Courtesy Dr Tillman Kohnert]

diagonal lines intersecting on the centre line. Others are formed of a pair of diagonal lines with a centre cross line, and some with two edge lines and a pair of crossed lines, creating a 'butterfly' design.

Nails and metalwork

Both the accounts and the structure show that large numbers of nails were used in the building, in fixing numerous smaller components but also structurally, and these merit some discussion in their own right. The account for 1426–7 notes expenditure on 250 spykenaylls, 350 fyfestrokenaylls, 6 gosefett, 6 woodcobbeleez and 12 hinges (*gumphis*).[216] Spykenaylls occur in numerous medieval accounts, the term specifying little more than large nails, although perhaps generally smaller than spikes;[217] fyfestrokenaylls were probably struck with five facets to the head, at least as suggested by the payment for 'nails with 5 strok hedes' in the 1470s cited by Salzman,[218] and the common use of such nails in pre-industrial buildings. The fact that the 208 nails to the plumb-cut top ends of the common rafters and the 52 fixing the 26 principal rafters to the arcade plate (two nails each) add up to 260, leaves little doubt that this was the destination of the spykenaylls;[219] the nails themselves are 125–150mm long, have square heads, are approximately 10mm across and 3–5mm thick.[220] Smaller nails with cruder, rounded heads, not mentioned in the accounts, were also used to fix the common rafter tops to the hip rafters – 28 per hip where observed at the north end, adding about 56 to the total number identified.[221]

The remaining nails and ironwork mentioned in the account were almost certainly fittings for the three doors. Gosefett or 'goosefeet' suggests three-pronged items, such as three-branched hinge straps. Assuming a consistently 'avian' terminology (and bearing in mind the old French *videcoq* for woodcock, the 'q' being silent), *wodecobbeleez* suggests 'woodcock bills' and thus long straight straps. Six of each would have provided a pair of both types for each leaf of the three double-leafed doors, each strap being hung on one of the twelve *gumphis* or pintles, an interpretation supported, in the sense of practicality, by the fact that the existing door leaves have two rather than three hinges each. Only one of the spoon-augered sockets for the original hinge pintles, however, is visible today, on the south jamb of the middle door, the rest being concealed by fillets nailed to the outer face of the jambs when the present doors were fitted, or, in the case of the upper ones, perhaps reused at that time. Hanging door-leafs with hinges of more than one form, including mixing straight and goosefoot types is a known medieval practice, found, for example, at the parish churches of Steyning (East Sussex), Castle Hedingham, Navestock, and Little Totham (Essex), and the hall door of *c* 1300 at Bisham Abbey (Berks).[222]

Given the carefully worked qualities of the fyfestrokenaylls, and that there were 350 of them, these too were probably also used for the doors, 58 on each leaf, perhaps fixing the boards to the ledgers in five rows of ten, allowing for some wastage and extra nails at points of stress; a nail of appropriate size, with a five-faceted head, survives part-driven into the upper surface of the collar to one of the southernmost trusses, and may be one of them. That such large numbers of nails were used in medieval doors is well known, an excellent parallel for Harmondsworth being the 500 large nails (*gross(i) clav(i)*) bought in 1406–7 for the two main doors of New College's new barn at Swalcliffe (Oxon), and the 150 nails later bought for the two small single-leaf doors in the opposite wall.[223] New College itself furnishes an interesting example in the 300 'white' nails (ie with tinned heads) bought in 1397 for 2s a hundred for the surviving 12ft-high double doors between the cloister and the bell tower.[224] Another example is afforded by the account for the building of Glastonbury Abbey's barn at Street (Somerset) in the early 1340s, where 800 nails were bought for the four leaves of the two 'big' barn doors and 500 for the 'smaller' ones.[225]

Two further categories of nail, not mentioned in the accounts, were also used: the small round-headed specimens fixing the boards to the barn walls, mentioned above, enough of which survive to show that they were roughly 4in (100mm) apart and must have numbered approximately 2,800, and the 40,000 nails – none of which have been securely identified on site – needed to fix the tile battens to the rafters.[226]

Roof covering

Reference to tilers (*tegulatores*) in the account for 1426–7, working under Roger Helyer, shows that the barn was originally tiled. Helyer, as mentioned above, received a £1 bonus on completion. His rate of pay is unknown but his men were paid 4d per day (*see* p 16), their work consisting not only of fixing the tiles but also the riven oak battens on which they were hung. The tiles themselves were clay peg tiles (pierced for latching on to the battens with 50–60mm wooden pegs), probably of the type found in the sill wall, 180mm wide and 15mm thick, the standard local medieval tile from the 13th century onwards.[227] The pegs must have resembled the 'tylepynnes' of which two bushels were brought from London in 1397–8.[228] The form of the roof would have required ridge tiles (*ryggetiell[s]*) and hip-tiles (*hopetiell[s]*), but not, in the absence of porches, any valley or gutter tiles (*gottertiell[s]*). The combination of abundant local sources of clay and nearby woodland, necessary for fuel, meant that the tiles could have come from a number of places: in 1386–7 they were brought from Burnham,[229] in 1397–8 from Harefield and Watford,[230] and in 1406–7 and 1451 from Ruislip, all within a radius of 14 miles.[231] Alternatively, they may have been made, or at least the clay dug, at Harmondsworth itself, as it was in 1433–4.[232]

The structural frame: oddities and significance

The timber frame at Harmondsworth, extraordinary in its size and state of preservation, displays a number of structural features which are unusual, innovative, backward, surprising or frankly inexplicable. First, the butt purlin joints to the principal rafter over the nave of the barn are formed of diminished haunched tenons arranged upside-down, with a barefaced tenon on the top of the purlin rather than at the bottom as a soffit tenon (Fig 13). This arrangement invites failure, as has happened here in a number of instances, as the diminished haunch makes no structural contribution, letting the load bear on the tenon alone, and is both extremely rare and hard to explain; only one other example is known, in the reused second-phase timbers of 1437–8 from the 303ft-long (92.35m) great barn at Cholsey (Oxon), demolished in 1811.[233] A better arrangement would have been to make the principal rafters wider, or set them below the plane of the rafters with a packing over.

Fig 13
Drawing showing the butt purlin assembly with diminished haunch tenon and (right) exploded to show construction. This is an early use of this arrangement, but the use of a tenon on the upper side of the timber, which has resulted in many purlins splitting under stress, as opposed to the much stronger arrangement with the tenon on the lower side, is puzzling. [Based on Kohnert 2012, 12 © Historic England Archive]

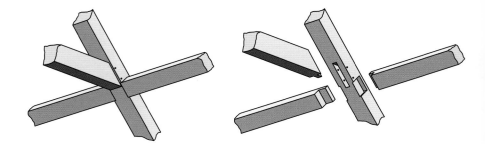

The reasons why a more structurally straightforward arrangement of clasped purlins was not used must lie in the method of assembly. However, inept as this arrangement may seem, the earliest identified conventional diminished haunch joint is found only a few years later, at 26 East St Helen's Street, Abingdon (Oxon), dated to 1429[234] and Blount's Court, Sonning Common (Oxon), of 1431. Thus, albeit upside-down, the Great Barn has the earliest diminished haunched tenon joints so far found in Britain.

Second, the Great Barn's roof structure includes crown struts (Fig 14) – both precocious and outside their usual geographical range. These are common in Buckinghamshire and South Oxfordshire in the mid-15th century. The earliest known, at Shepherd's Cottage, North Warnborough (Hants) dates from 1402,[235] followed by another Hampshire example from 1401–20, and five others in the period 1440–60.[236] Other early examples date from 1443 at the barn at Burrow Farm, Hambledon (Bucks) and the Long Gallery, Abingdon Abbey (Oxon) (1455) and in Henley-on-Thames (Oxon) (15th century). In addition, the aisle purlin is clasped by a raking strut which is itself an early example, these being more commonly found in the 16th century.[237]

Third, it is interesting that the setting-out of the main trusses used the French centre line rather than the English scribe or fair-face method.[238] In the former, the centre line of each timber (ie a line mid-way between its edges) was used as the point to measure from in relating it, in two dimensions (ie when laid out on the ground),

Fig 14
A crown strut – the vertical timber between the tie beam (below) and the collar. This is an unusual feature in the early 15th century and used here outside its normal geographical range. The diagonal timbers to right and left are later insertions.
[Courtesy Dr Tillman Kohnert]

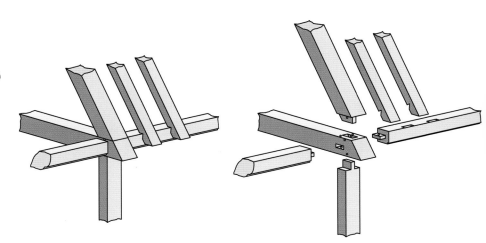

to the other timbers of the truss: in the latter, carpenters usually measured from the edges of each timber.

The centre-line method has practical advantages in allowing greater accuracy of setting out, as hewn faces (as opposed to sawn) can be irregular, unlike a straight centre line drawn or strung out on the timber. Greater accuracy also allows for some standardisation of the joints, since mortices and tenons could be cut to standard dimensions and be expected to fit at the moment of assembly, rather than being cut, tried, and adjusted during the setting-out.

The fourth, and perhaps the most unusual feature of the framing, is the configuration of the aisle wall-plates, which are neither normal nor reversed assembly (ie with the aisle ties either sitting on the plates or fitted below them), but instead are tenoned into the sides of the aisle ties, as with a butt purlin (Fig 15). This, it seems, is the earliest known occurrence of this arrangement in Britain. It is surprising, however, that the only structural members tying the structure together lengthwise, apart from the sill beams, are the aisle purlins and the arcade plates, made up of timbers of varying length scarfed together: at the tops of the walls, where this additional strength would have been particularly valuable, the plates are not continuous but butted against the sides of the aisle ties.

Fifth, the survival of so much of the external vertical boarding (Fig 16) is also of interest. This was used in the mid-13th century barn at Belchamp St Paul (Essex), as identified from reused components,[239] and in the large Kentish barns at Littlebourne (1307–27) and Frindsbury (1404).[240] In the latter cases the boards are retained in a rebate in the sill beam and, interestingly, secured to the middle rails by wedged pegs. This would suggest that vertical boarding, as found at Harmondsworth, was not a rarity among medieval timber barns, at least those of comparable quality and scale.

Sixth, the longitudinal twisting of the frame resulting from the poor levelling of the sill walls, and its use of large nails instead of pegs to fix the aisle rafters and principal rafters to the arcade plate.

Overall, then, the carpentry of the barn is, paradoxically, both innovative and naïve. Could it be that Kyppyng, or whoever it was who designed the building, lacking experience on projects of this scale, made some mistakes, but also either invented, or applied in an innovative way, a number of structural details not found elsewhere at this date? Or can the mixture of relative incompetence with forward thinking be explained by mixed command, change of command, or some other recipe for human error? Either way, the Great Barn at Harmondsworth occupies a puzzling and interesting place in the history of timber framing in England.

Building sequence

The detailing of the building's carpentry also allows for speculation as to the order in which the main components were assembled. While a number of interpretations are possible – and one is given below – they all need to be consistent with the following structural features.

First, the full-width cross frames – comprising arcade posts, aisle cross frames and nave roof trusses – could not have been raised as single pre-assembled units because the arcade plates, some of which span more than one bay, are integral to the structure of the cross frames. The arcade plates are trapped in the joints between the arcade posts and the nave roof truss tiebeams which means that, in the sequence of construction, the arcade plate had to be located on top of the arcade post before the tiebeam was put in place.

Second, it is unlikely that each arcade post and its associated aisle cross frame was reared as a complete pre-assembled unit, as the principal rafters above the aisles could not have been installed until the aisle purlin was clasped between the raking strut and the notched-out principal rafter.

Third, it is equally unlikely that the arcades with their arcade plates and braces were raised up towards the centre of the building in continuous, pre-assembled, 192ft-long units since it would have have required an unfeasibly enormous workforce (Fig 17).

Fig 17

Schematic elevations viewed from the east of both the east and west arcades, illustrating the joints, the sequence in which the arcade plates (shown in brown) were laid (the earliest being at the bottom) and how the work was probably undertaken by three gangs. [Richard Lea]

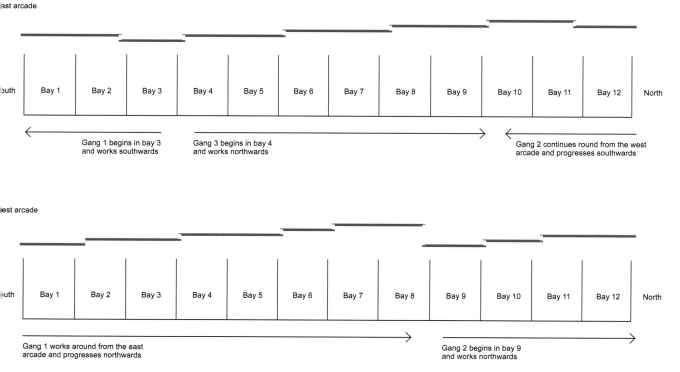

east arcade

| South | Bay 1 | Bay 2 | Bay 3 | Bay 4 | Bay 5 | Bay 6 | Bay 7 | Bay 8 | Bay 9 | Bay 10 | Bay 11 | Bay 12 | North |

Gang 1 begins in bay 3 and works southwards

Gang 3 begins in bay 4 and works northwards

Gang 2 continues round from the west arcade and progresses southwards

west arcade

| South | Bay 1 | Bay 2 | Bay 3 | Bay 4 | Bay 5 | Bay 6 | Bay 7 | Bay 8 | Bay 9 | Bay 10 | Bay 11 | Bay 12 | North |

Gang 1 works around from the east arcade and progresses northwards

Gang 2 begins in bay 9 and works northwards

The most probable sequence – although others could be inferred from the same evidence – is described in detail in the drawings and captions in Fig 18, and has been identified on the basis of the following observations:

a) A few lengths of aisle purlin span one bay only but most of the others span two. They are scarf jointed with the joints located over the raking struts. The directions of the scarf joints indicate that they were installed beginning at the south end of the barn and continuing north.

b) The tiebeams across the nave must have been placed individually once the arcades were erected. With the tiebeams in place, the remaining aisle truss elements as well as the main roof trusses could be assembled one member at a time.

c) The wall frames could be assembled one bay at a time because the aisle wall plates were contained within each bay. The main nave roof could be erected one truss at a time and, similarly, the nave purlins with their diminished haunched tenons could be added one bay at a time. The only other longitudinal roof members are the aisle purlins which were mostly assembled two bays at a time, by nestling or clasping the notched raking strut and lowering the aisle principal rafter down onto the joint, thereby locking the purlin into place. So the building was probably erected one bay at a time, piece by piece.

d) The scarf joints in the arcade plates and their locations provide evidence for the sequence of construction. The bridled arcade plate scarf joint is a simple hybrid combining characteristics of a mortice and tenon with a half lap joint. At Harmondsworth, in the two halves of the joint the tenoned part is consistently used on top of its morticed counterpart. Within the additive sequence of construction, the arcade plates must have been lowered onto the arcade posts and each tenoned arcade plate must have been lowered onto an adjacent morticed section. The arcade plates above bay 3 in the east arcade and bay 9 in the west arcade are similar; their ends, which project slightly into the adjacent bays, are cut with upward facing joints. They therefore appear to be the earliest in the sequence of construction, and because they suggest two starting places, that the work was undertaken by more than one gang of workmen.

e) The sequence suggested by this analysis appears to begin in bay 3 of the east arcade. The two ends of the arcade plate above bay 3 have upward facing joints to receive further plates to north and south. If this was the work of the first gang, it probably then moved south, completing the south end of the barn before proceeding north along the west arcade. Before this gang had reached bay 8 of the west arcade, a second gang had already begun bay 9 of the same arcade, capping it with an arcade plate cut with upward facing joints at each end like that above bay 3 in the east arcade. This second gang then worked northwards, completing the north end of the barn before assembling bay 12. A third gang was probably responsible for bays 4 to 9 in the east arcade, working north from the bay assembled by the first gang. Bays 10 and 11 in the east arcade might have been completed by either the second or third gang.

Stage 1. Once the masonry plinths and sill wall were complete, the sill beams and aisle sills could be set in place, either one bay at a time or all at once. The aisle sills are tenoned into the sides of the sill beams, which are composed of various lengths of timber scarf-jointed together. Those on the west wall are relatively uniform in length, each spanning two bays, while those in the east wall, interrupted by door openings, are shorter. Some sections on the east wall have been repaired or replaced. The use of scarf joints on the west wall suggests that the sill beams were laid from south to north. The sequence on the east side is harder to see because of the complications caused by alteration.

Stage 2. With the aisle sills in place, the arcade posts could be located within mortices in the aisle sills.

Stage 3. With the arcade posts in place, the wall posts, aisle braces and wall frames could be installed. The scarf joints in the arcade plates suggest that bay 3, around the south door, was the first in the sequence (*see* Stage 6). In this bay, the wall is pierced by a door frame composed of full-height door posts tied to the wall post by rails.

Stage 4. The aisle ties and wall plate could then be set into the arcade post while being lowered on to the tenons of the aisle and wall frames.

Stage 5. The arcade braces could then be installed in readiness for the arcade plate.

Stage 6. The arcade plate could then be lowered onto the tenons on the arcade posts and arcade braces. Both ends of the arcade plate, which extended beyond the arcade posts into the adjacent bays, were dressed with the upward facing morticed half of a scarf joint. Arcade plates in both of the adjacent bays could then be lowered onto this section of the plate while also being lowered on to the adjacent arcade posts.

Stage 7. With the first bay assembled, work could progress either to the north or south. In the sequence suggested here, work moved to the south, beginning with the sill beams.

Stage 8. The assembly could then progress according to the pattern established in the first bay with the arcade post being installed first.

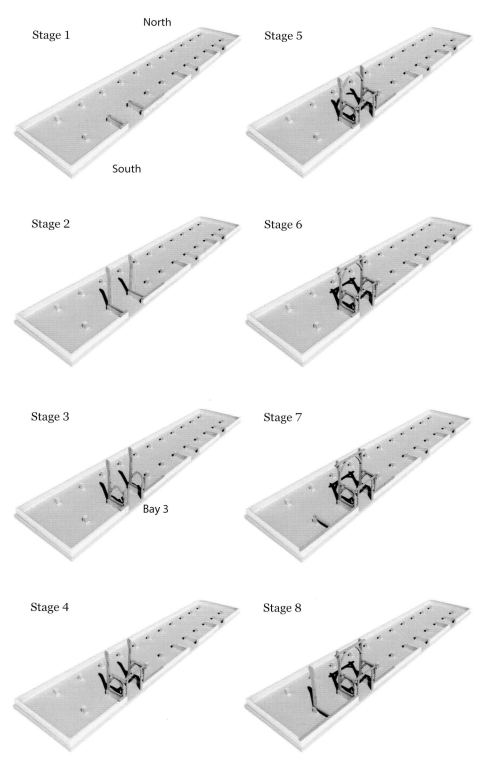

Fig 18 continued

Stage 9. The aisle and wall frames could then follow.

Stage 10. The addition of aisle ties and wall plates would have allowed the creation of a temporary platform which would have been useful during the assembly of the upper parts of the arcade and nave roof. The installation of the arcade braces would have been facilitated by such a platform.

Stage 11. Before the arcade plate that spans both bays 1 and 2 could be added, the arcade post, brace, aisle frame and wall frame in bay 1 had to be assembled.

Stage 12. The assembly of the south end wall frame meant that work could progress at the south end of the west aisle.

Stage 13. The arcade plate above the south bay of the west aisle extended into the second bay. The scarf joint at its north end differs from the other scarf joints in missing its upper lap. However, the tenon of the next arcade plate to the north could still be let down into its mortice.

Stage 14. Once the two southern aisle bays were complete and the arcade plates had been put in place, the tie beams and the nave roof truss could be installed. The nave trusses including their tie beams may have been pre-assembled before erection.

Stage 15. Working bay by bay, the assembly could then progress northwards along the west aisle.

Stage 16. The first element in the assembly of the hipped roof above the southern bay of the nave was probably the half-height collar braced truss set below the gablet. The diagonal principals of the hip rest on the purlins which in turn are supported by the half-height truss.

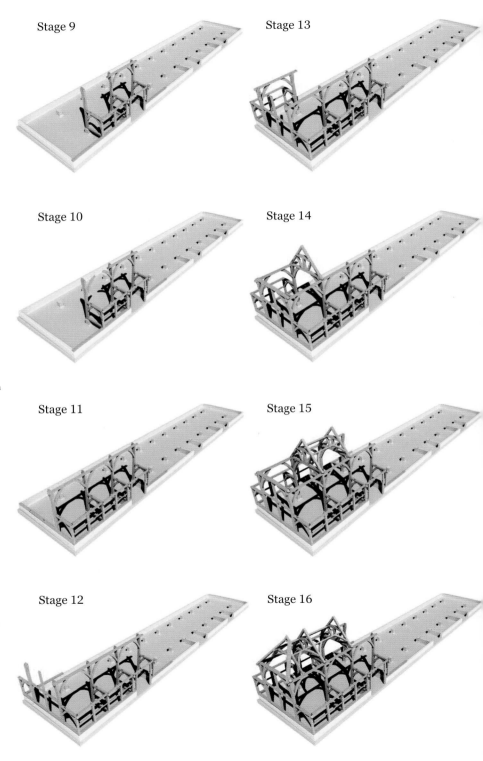

Stage 9

Stage 10

Stage 11

Stage 12

Stage 13

Stage 14

Stage 15

Stage 16

Fig 18 continued

Stage 17. With more than one gang on site, assembly may well have proceeded northwards in both aisles.

Stage 18. At the same time, a second or third gang may have been working on the west aisle towards the north end of the barn beginning in bay 9. Like that above bay 3 in the east aisle, the arcade plate above bay 8 extended into the adjacent bays with mortices ready to receive arcade plates lowered into place to north and south.

Stage 19. This gang probably then proceeded northwards.

Stage 20. As with the work at the south end, the northern gang probably worked around the end wall of the barn.

Stage 21. Meanwhile, work could progress in both aisles from the south.

Stage 22. The gaps between the work of the southern and northern gangs were infilled with arcade plates. These had scarf tenons at each end which could be lowered onto their morticed counterparts.

Stage 23. With the arcades complete, the roof trusses could be installed above the nave. Again, use may well have been made of temporary platforms erected above the aisle framing.

Stage 24. The jointing of the purlins suggests that the aisle roof trusses were then added by working from the south.

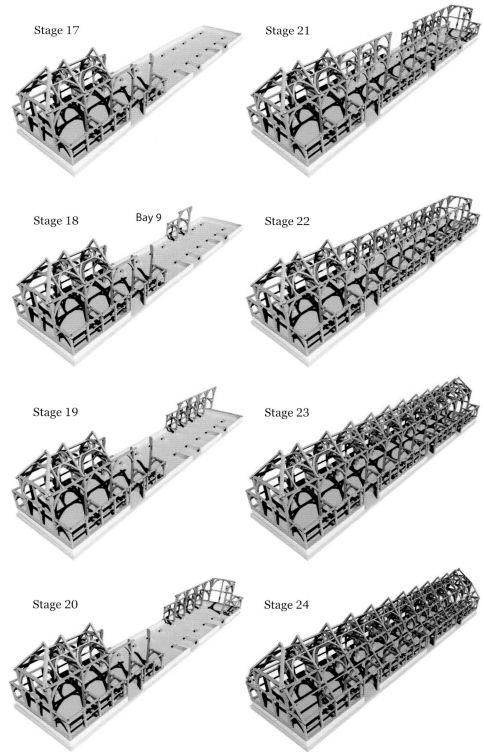

Stage 17

Stage 18   Bay 9

Stage 19

Stage 20

Stage 21

Stage 22

Stage 23

Stage 24

Changes of plan

The timber frame reveals several changes of plan during construction, the most significant being to the positions of the two northern doorways, in bays 7 and 10, but originally intended, respectively, for bays 8 and 11. This is shown by the pieced-in sills, the fixing of the central studs to the sill beam and the rails in both by use of slip tenons, and the empty mortices in the underside of the aisle wall plates, clearly intended to house the door jambs. Below, the masonry sill wall was evidently built from the start to accommodate doorways in bays 8 and 11 in their existing positions. The explanation is presumably that the carpenters (initially, perhaps, working off site) and the masons unintentionally placed the doorways in different bays, but when assembling the building it was deemed less trouble to alter the frame than to rebuild the wall; possibly craft rivalries and antagonisms, particularly the medieval mason's disdain for carpenters, may have played a part.[241] It is puzzling, however, that the mismatch seems not to have been noticed or attended to until the main elements of the frame were in place, as otherwise they could simply have fitted the central studs and rails intended for bays 8 and 11 to bays 7 and 10, without the need for slip-tenons.

Other irregularities include redundant mortices in the connecting cross sill beams between the aisle sill plates and arcade posts 7, 8, 9, 10 and 12 on the east side, and 8, 9 and 12 on the west side. The HAWK Institute group noted during their study in 2012 that some of these empty mortices were filled with blocks of oak, of a similar type and appearance to that of the original structure. It is not known what these mortices had been intended for, although McCurdy suggests that they had simply been cut on the wrong side of the main arcade setting-out line. There is also a series of auger holes for an uncut mortice adjacent to the west arcade post of truss 10. These errors occur on pairs of arcade posts from four trusses, with the exception of truss 7, and suggest that one inexperienced carpenter was responsible for this mistake, and was only caught when he had started on the west side of truss 10. McCurdy also noted two redundant mortices in the east aisle purlin in bay 3 for which he could find no explanation.

Another interesting mistake was made in the west aisle wall frame in bay 1 where the centre stud appears to have been cut about 2 inches short, overcome by pegging a packing piece to the underside of the aisle wall plate into which the stud was tenoned and pegged.

Pegging also seems to be a little variable, in that a number of arcade braces on the west side of bays 3 through 7 were not pegged to the arcade plate, although the holes had been drilled. It was also noted by McCurdy that some of the arcade braces were flushed up on the outside of the arcade posts while others were offset by an inch or two.

Repairs and modifications

Although so impressively original, the barn has of course been subject to numerous repairs since its completion – many very minor ones, fewer substantial ones.[242] These include work to the sill wall, the most substantial being to the eastern wall at bays 5–6, where roughly 2m of it has been wholly rebuilt, reusing ferricrete blocks, some early post-medieval bricks and others of 18th- or 19th-century type: these, and the reuse of massive Reigate blocks which Drury plausibly suggests 'are most likely the aisle post plinth blocks'[243] from the formerly adjacent barn of 1434–5 (demolished between 1795 and 1816), probably date the work to the early 19th century.

Successive re-coverings of the roof apart, the last of which was in the late 1950s,[244] the most extensive work to the timber framing has been the insertion of seven hatches in the west wall, four with double doors, above the mid rail (bays 2, 5, 8, 11), and three with one door below (bays 5, 7, 10). These are clearly insertions, as the rebate which housed the 14th-century cladding boards continues over the openings, and the hinges, although in all but one case hand-made, suggest an 18th- or early 19th-century origin. In one case (bay 2) the boards are elm and probably original to the hatch, but the others are all softwood and of varying dates. They may have been intended to let in extra light for threshing, and perhaps draught, and by the mid-20th century (and so perhaps for a century or so before) were being used for pitching sheaves out of the barn for machine-threshing outside, and also for loading potatoes and roots into the building.[245] At some stage after the mid-1860s but before c 1920, large hatches or doors were opened in the north wall, one above wall-plate level and one below, still present c 1950.[246] The single door to the south elevation, certainly there by 1935 but destroyed and not replaced in 1972, was perhaps of the same date. Many of the cover strips to the medieval cladding pre-date the first tarring of the exterior in about 1830.[247] Numerous minor repairs and ironwork reinforcements have been carried out over a long period, including to the split jowls of the southern arcade posts (trusses 4 and 5), frequently using, as usual in this kind of work, sections of reused iron cart tyre.

The most significant repairs, however, belong to the 20th century and since. In 1943, £88 10s was spent on repairs to the roof and eaves boarding following storm damage, and the expedient structural work, since reversed, of 'taking out rotten plate and filling with concrete and cutting off rotten ends of posts and framing, and renewing with concrete stooling'.[248] More significantly, in 1972 the south end of the barn (bay 1) was damaged by fire,[249] the necessary repairs being aided by a 50 per cent grant of £4,000 by the Historic Buildings Council.[250] Further repairs were effected in 1988–9 by McCurdy and Co, including the replacement of the sill to the north end, and by the same firm in 1991,[251] accompanied and guided by a remarkably detailed hand-drawn survey made the previous year.[252] The most extensive repair scheme in its history, however, was that carried out by English Heritage after the purchase of the barn in 2011, described below (p 63).

Using the Great Barn

Essential purposes

The purpose of barns such as Harmondsworth's was to store the main produce of the manorial demesne, ie the land retained by the lord to exploit for his own purposes: grain produced by the peasants of the manor on their own land, whether free or unfree, was stored separately in their own barns.[253] At the time of the Great Barn's construction, and indeed throughout and beyond the Middle Ages, demesne land could be exploited in one of two ways. It could be cultivated directly on the lord's behalf, in which case it had to be worked by hired labour, or through the labour services owed by the unfree peasants of the manor, and overseen by the lord's officials. Alternatively the demesne could be leased or 'farmed' – rented en bloc from the landlord by a tenant in return for a fixed annual payment.[254] Barns such as Harmondsworth's were used to store either the corn of the lord or the lessee, depending on the managerial regime of the time. In the case of Harmondsworth, large-scale demesne farming seems to have been practiced unbroken from the 13th century, barring periods from 1294 to 1392 when managed by a government agent, and for three years in the early 15th century,[255] until as late as 1456–7.[256] In a national context this was unusual as, generally speaking, the demesne system had been giving way to 'farming' since the peak of direct cultivation in *c* 1300, although among monastic and collegiate institutions, such as Winchester, with standing bureaucracies and sizeable static households, at a slower rate;[257] Middlesex manors in general also appear to have been slow to move to leasing.[258] According to the accepted classification of demesne management by Bruce Campbell *et al* into seven types, according to the range and balance of all agricultural activities, late 14th- and early 15th-century Harmondsworth fell into one of the three 'mixed farming' categories; only the outlier at Ruislip, with its abundant woodland, may have belonged to a different category 'arable husbandry with swine'.[259] With the leasing of the demesne from 1456–7, the lessees and tenants continued, singly or severally, to use the great barn to store their crops.

Contrary to popular myth and the name attached to it since at least the early 20th century,[260] the Great Barn was not, as has been noted above, a 'tithe barn'. Barns specifically for tithe storage do appear in medieval manorial documents, including those relating to Harmondsworth itself. These could be required at sites where the lord was both proprietor and corporate rector – as at Harmondsworth and most episcopal, monastic or collegiate manors, to house a tenth of both the manorial tenants' own produce – or, where warranted by their volume, tithe takings of an unappropriated rectory. Examples of the former, both properties of the dean and chapter of St Paul's, include the tithe barn (*grangia decimae)* recorded at Barling (Essex) in 1281, quite distinct from the adjacent great barn (*magna grangia)*, or the building 'for the storage of the manor's tithes' (*ad reponendum decimas ville)* at nearby Drayton (Middlesex) in 1294–1304.[261] Where tithe barns existed, they stored every tenth sheaf of grain from every parishioner with corn to give, including that of other lords in the parish. When and whether such barns also stored tithes from the demesne is less clear. In the case of Harmondsworth there is a hint that all tithes were indeed stored separately, in the actions of the recalcitrant customary tenant Roger Cook, who in 1399 threw part of his cartload of sheaves on the 'tithe stack' and the rest on the ground,[262] if only in suggesting that his cartload of demesne produce had two destinations – a 'tithe stack' and, by implication a separate demesne stack. Normally speaking, however, and probably at Harmondsworth, labour and trouble were saved by taking all the demesne crops into the demesne barn without separating the tithe.[263] As perpetual rector, the college could dispose of the tithes of the parish, including the demesne tithes, as it saw fit, although tithes were, generally speaking, intended for fairly specific purposes, which would make this separation logical. Given the proportion of the total crop they were intended to store, tithe barns tended to be smaller than their demesne counterparts, as was the case at Harmondsworth (Table 2), although exceptions could presumably occur if the proportion of tenanted land to demesne was particularly high.[264]

The practical need for both demesne and tithe barns was dictated, essentially, by the need for safe and dry storage of the cereal crop during the long process of extracting the grain. As remained the case well into the 20th century in England, medieval farmers also stored sheaves in ricks,[265] thatched and sometimes raised off the ground, and this must have been so at Harmondsworth: a rickyard is mentioned several times, as is, in 1397–8, the cost of five days' work thatching a 'great stack' of peas,[266] although cornstacks are nowhere specifically mentioned. But while avoiding the capital outlay required by a barn, rick-building was relatively slow and expensive and the grain risked spoilage once the rick was 'opened'.[267] Ricks were also exposed to theft, whereas barns could be locked.[268] As a result, ricks were generally used only at places or in years when indoor space was insufficient. As shown by the 13th-century custumal and later accounts,[269] the barn or barns at Harmondsworth were also used for storing crops of peas, beans and hay: these too could be stored in ricks, and for

Table 2 Quantities of wheat produced at Harmondsworth 'answered for' by the bailiffs and recorded in the four last surviving accounts

Year	Bailiff	Wheat (demesne)	Wheat (tithe)
1397–8	John Laner	1444 bushels (best)	
1406–7	Nicholas Cranmor	574 bushels (best)	206 (best)
		300 bushels (poor)	64 (poor)
		Total: 874 bushels	**Total: 270**
1433–4	Roger Hubbard	892 bushels (best)	112 (best)
		532 bushels (poor)	33 (poor)
		Total: 1424	**Total: 145**
1450–1	John Hubbard	1282 bushels (best)	240.5 (best)
		309 bushels (poor)	64 (poor)
		Total: 1591	**Total: 304.5**

Note the difference in the figures, indicating that the bailiffs were recording actual annual production, not a pre-agreed charge, and the quantities issued of the demesne barn compared to those of the tithe barn.

hay this was the normal method. Barns also had an important function in providing covered space for threshing and winnowing the crop before transfer, as clean grain, to the granary – processes that are described below.

Sources

The main sources for understanding all aspects of the barn's functioning are the manorial accounts. In addition to being the key source of quantitative information about the manor's productivity, they also reveal a good deal of the systems used to track the processing, use and distribution of the crop. The purpose of the accounting system used at Harmondsworth was to assure the college, the corporate lord of the manor, that the manor was being properly run on its behalf by the bailiff, its chief local official, and to enumerate the manor's annual costs and income in cash, kind and services, and identify the balance. The documents took the form of accounts (*compoti*), following a format devised in the 13th century, although the Harmondsworth examples belong to a more advanced form described by Paul Harvey as 'Phase 2', typically current from the mid-13th to the mid-14th century,[270] but retained at Harmondsworth into at least the 1450s, thanks to its late retention of demesne farming. Harmondsworth *compoti*, or the essentials of their texts, survive for the years 1323–4 and 1386–7 (ie before Wykeham's purchase), and, from the years of the college's ownership, for 1388–9, 1397–8, 1406–7, 1433–4 and 1450–1; the last two sets, of course, relate to the period in which the existing Great Barn was in use. These accounts cover a financial year from Michaelmas (29 September) to the Michaelmas of the following year, and their arrangement follows a roughly standardised format, based on the principle of 'charge' and 'discharge', the charge identifying and valuing what was expected from, or produced by, the bailiff, and the 'discharge' accounting for the uses to which it was put. Particularly in cases where what was expected of the bailiff each year was fixed, the arrangement was, in practice, close to that of lord and 'farmer' when an estate was leased for a fixed annual sum, but at Harmondsworth the bailiff 'answered for' different quantities of produce in each financial year, and the figure must therefore have represented the fact of the matter rather than a target (Table 2).

There is also the complication, where the accounts deal with cereal production, that while all expenditure listed took place within the financial year in question, the harvest which produced the grain being answered for and expended was that of the previous financial year: thus, the account for September 1433 to September 1434 describes what happened to the harvest of (depending on the crop) July–September 1433; the 'costs of the harvest', meanwhile, which such accounts routinely enumerate, are those for the September of the second year, but paid for with, or with the receipts from, the previous harvest.

The format of the accounts was fairly standard, listing first 'costs of the harvest' (ie the harvest of the previous financial year but accounted for in the next), paid in cash and in grain. The quantities of each type of grain that the bailiff 'should answer for' (*respondet*), ie the 'charge', were listed; thus, in 1433–4, for example, the demesne produced 166 quarters and 1 bushel of barley; then, under each crop type, what it was used for or to whom it was made over (the 'discharge'), in the case of the barley crop of 1433, for seed and given to doves, horses and pigs, and (the largest quantity) sold.[271] As the quantity charged equalled that discharged the item is closed (*Summa que supra. Et eque*; 'Total as above. And equal'). By way of illustration the charges and discharges itemised in the 1433–4 account are summarised in Table 3.

Officials and their roles

The operation of the routines and processes surrounding the use of the great barn at Harmondsworth required careful organisation, division of labour and allocation of authority, and the names of many of the officials and individuals involved are known, along with the occasional hint about their personalities. The most important sources are the documents specific to Winchester and Harmondsworth, especially the accounts described above, and, in relation to its overall administrative structure, the college's statutes.[272] But in addition to the help of abundant secondary literature on the subject, our understanding of how Harmondsworth was managed is enhanced by a number of medieval treatises on estate management and accounting. The most important of these are the anonymous *Seneschaucy*, written a little before 1276, Walter of Henley's *Husbandry* (hereafter called *Walter*) of 1286, the *Rules* derived from Robert Grosseteste's famous advice to the Countess of Lincoln (1240–2), and the anonymous *Husbandry* of later in the century.[273] Although significantly earlier than the Great Barn, and written at the height of demesne farming, when larger acreages were generally worked in this way than in the early 15th century, much of the processes and practices they describe, in relation to arable farming, can be recognised at Harmondsworth.

At the head of the college was the warden, ultimately responsible for all aspects of its success and prosperity, including its educational and pastoral functions: at the time of the Great Barn's construction, the warden was Walter Thurbern (1413–50).[274] The senior official in charge of the college's landed property and interests was the *senescallus* (steward), a layman, not a fellow, and almost always a lawyer,[275] although the responsibility was sometimes split between two of them: he or they was/were supported by a number of clerks.[276] The actual revenues of the manors were received, safeguarded and documented by a pair of the ten permanent fellows of the college appointed annually to serve as bursars (*bursarii*);[277] it is from the account of Robert Heate and Richard Boureman, bursars in 1424–5, that we know about the Great Barn's inception.[278] At the time of Wykeham's purchase, the steward was probably William Pope (certainly in office 1394–1404), and from 1405 until 1414 William Stokes was steward for the Middlesex and Berkshire manors. When the Great Barn was being built, the steward of all Winchester's estates was Richard Wallop (1413–30), although in 1429–30 the stewardship of Middlesex was held separately by William Sydney.[279] Far from being remote bureaucrats, the stewards were regular visitors of the college manors, on local business, and in the case of Harmondsworth, en route between

Table 3 Charges and discharges related to cereal production at Harmondsworth, 1433–34

Item	Charge (quantity of product recorded)	Discharge (use of product)	Discharge (totals in bushels)
Wheat		Sowing of 106 acres, 264 bushels annual payment to bailiff, 52 bushels; in payment to beadle and others, 416 bushels; bread baked for the harvest, 40 bushels; payment to smith, 2 bushels; payment to William Appleby, *contratalliator*, 2 bushels; 'In gift to the lord and to a certain servant of the king', 10 bushels; sold, 824 bushels; 'and beyond this account' (*super compotum*) 2 bushels and 1 peck (ie a deficit or excess discharge).[a]	**1611 bushels**
Wheat (demesne)	892 bushels		
Poor wheat (demesne)	572 bushels		
Wheat (tithe)	112 bushels		
Poor wheat (tithe)	33 bushels 1 peck		
Sub Total	**1609 bushels 1 peck**		
Curallum	**120 bushels**	Fed to horses: 120 bushels	**120 bushels**
Barley		Sown, 320 bushels; to William Appleby, 8 bushels; to a sower, 1 bushel; for pig food, 25 bushels; sold, 960 bushels; malted, 160 bushels; 'and beyond this account 3 quarters 2.5 bushels (ie 26 bushels 2 pecks) for 17s 6d'[b]	**1467 bushels**
Barley (demesne)	1249 bushels		
Barley (tithe)	182 bushels		
Barley (heaping, tithe and demesne)	44 bushels		
super compotum	24 bushels		
Sub Total	**1499 bushels**		
Harascum (barns not differentiated)	**482 bushels**	Sown, 100 bushels; fed to doves, 4 bushels; fed to horses and pigs, 80 bushels; sold, 298 bushels; 'Total as above and equal'	**482 bushels**
Oats (barns not differentiated)	**166 bushels**	Sown, 44 bushels; feeding the horses of the warden [of Winchester], 7½ bushels; feeding the warden's horses in his absence, 18 bushels; feeding Sir Richard Beryman's horses and John Godwyn's, 1 bushel; for feeding the horses of the steward, clerk and other officers, 6 bushels; for feeding the sheriff of Middlesex's horses, 8 bushels; feeding plough-horses, 4 bushels; for feeding servants, 40 bushels; sold, 9½ bushels. And upon this account 2 quarters for 4s. 'Total as above and equal'	**154 bushels**
Barley for malt	**165 bushels**	Ale brewed for the harvest, 136 bushels; sold, 21 bushels. 'Total as above and equal'	**165 bushels**
TOTAL	**4041 bushels 1 peck**		**3999 bushels**

a   The excess as calculated in 1434 (2 bushels, 1 peck) and as calculated today on the basis of the account (1 bushel, 3 pecks) could be accounted for by errors of calculation – now and then, of transcription, or in the original figures themselves.

b   For the differences between the charge–discharge of 26 bushels 2 pecks as calculated in 1434 and between the total of 32 bushels as calculated today, see note above.

Winchester and London: the account for 1433–4 records the six bushels of grain 'for the feeding of the horses of the steward (Thomas Haydock), a clerk and others coming there to hold courts and other business',[280] and those of 1450–1 for making similar provision for the steward Edmund Brokenell and his entourage.[281]

At the time of purchase, the senior officer on site was the bailiff, then still probably Thomas atte Rydyngge,[282] but the college's first appointee was probably John Laner (or Laver), bailiff from at least as early as 1394–5 until 1403–4.[283] After a brief vacancy in the latter part of 1403–4 (*tempore vacacionis ballivi*), requiring the temporary appointment of Stephen Ansteswell,[284] the post was occupied in 1405–6 and 1406–7 by Nicholas Cranmore,[285] from 1407–8 to at least 1412–13 by William Tyghale,[286] and from 1413–14 to 1420–1 by John Mayhew, except for John Okebourne's tenure in 1415–16.[287] Thereafter the bailiffs were members of the Hubbard family – Roger from 1421–2 until 1447–8,[288] and John from that year until 1454–5, after which the manor was farmed and John appears as 'former bailiff'.[289] The background and duties of the Harmondsworth bailiffs, as the Winchester documents show, are much as prescribed in the *Walter* and the *Seneschaucy*: they were appointed for terms that were probably undefined but, as in the case of the Hubbards, could endure for many years; payment was made partly in kind (6 quarters 4 bushels of wheat in 1433–4), and partly in cash (£2 in that year).[290] In 1424–5 and 1430–1, the college paid Roger Hubbard a bonus by way of a yard of cloth, given to his wife, the material in the latter year being 'coloured'.[291] In 1450–1 a bailiff's chamber (*camera ballivi*) in the manor house is mentioned, containing a wooden bed, an iron-bound chest, a worn basin and large jug (broken), showing that accommodation was also provided, if only for the bailiff himself and presumably for use during peak periods of work.[292] The space may also have served him as an office, as has been suggested of the chamber, equipped with fireplace and latrine, above the south-east porch of the barn at Bredon (Worcs). The chamber over the west porch at Great Coxwell, removed in the 18th century, may have had a similar function.[293]

Thomas atte Rydyngge and John atte Nasshes and their successors under the college were also its tenants,[294] and may have had some familiarity, as the treatises imply that they should, with the law, and have been literate in French, although the manorial documents were probably prepared by a professional clerk;[295] some manorial bailiffs were drawn from the lesser gentry,[296] although not in any known instance at Harmondsworth, and perhaps more commonly when in charge of more than one manor. In any case, their authority and duties were substantial, being responsible to the lord for managing the manor and acting as its accounting officer.[297] Success would certainly have required all the attributes of Chaucer's reeve Oswald (in fact occupying a role equivalent to the Winchester bailiffs), of whom we are told:

> He kept his bins and garners very trim;
> No auditor could gain a point on him.
> And he could judge by watching drought and rain
> The yield he might expect from seed and grain.[298]

Working for the bailiff, at the time of the Great Barn's construction, was the beadle (*bedellus* in the Harmondsworth accounts), mentioned but not named in 1388–9,[299] 1397–8,[300] 1406–7,[301] 1433–4[302] and 1450–1;[303] he was, effectively, the foreman and rent-collector, and he too was a manorial tenant, in this case appointed or re-appointed annually by the tenantry and rewarded in kind and by remission of rents and services. At this time it was common practice for a hayward, responsible for mustering the customary tenants and other duties, to report to the bailiff,[304] although in the case of Harmondsworth this office (*messorius*) is mentioned only in 1403–4,[305] 1433–4, and 1450–1, in which year the post was held jointly with that of the beadle;[306] in 1433–4 he received a stipend of 16s.[307] In 1397–8, uniquely, a reap-reeve (*rypereeve*) was recorded at Harmondsworth, a certain William Holdare,[308] but the post must normally have been filled, as in 1406–7 it was noted that no payment was made 'this year because there is no reap-reeve there'.[309] A granger (*grangiator*) called William in control of filling and emptying the barn is mentioned in 1388–9, and in 1397–8 he was William Cauche, perhaps the same man;[310] in some years, even perhaps normally, this task may have been taken on by the bailiff.[311] Standard practice would also have required a granary-keeper (*granetarius* or *granator*), a role not mentioned by title in the Harmondsworth accounts but which may have been fulfilled by the beadle. The manor employed the services of a tallier (*talliator*) and tally-checker (*contratalliator*), William Senton holding the latter position in 1406–7[312] and William Appulby in 1433–4.[313] These officials were probably itinerant, arriving at Harmondsworth at harvest-time and at other moments to check or audit the records of crop and grain movements and transactions, processes described in more detail below.

Crops, harvesting and filling the barns

Harmondsworth's single most important product of direct relevance to the Great Barn was wheat, of which, for example, 108 acres of demesne were sown in 1406–7, as opposed to a total of 125 acres of other crops and cereals.[314] Part of the wheat crop (as in 1406–7, 1450–1 and 1433–4), however, was classed in the records as *curallum*, ie, smaller and broken grains separated by sieving:[315] the distinction is borne out by the 1406–7 account, which records that the whole 19 quarters 7 bushels and 1 peck of *curallum* issued from both the demesne barn and the tithe barn was 'given to the pigs, young sheep, piglets and poultry and also to the pigeons in winter';[316] it was never sown.[317] Barley (*ordeum*), oats (*avena*), and a mixed fodder crop of oats and legumes (peas, beans and/or vetches) called *harascum*,[318] and separate crops of pulses (peas and/or beans) made up the rest of the harvest (Table 4). Finally, there was the hay crop, part of which, as in 1433–4, was stored in the 'lord's barn', a reference either to the Great Barn or the hay barn, also the lord's. The various crops were sown and harvested at marginally different times, and wheat, as now, was sown both in the late autumn ('winter wheat') in time for it to sprout before winter and the early spring ('spring wheat'), to spread the risk of poor or failed crops. Barley was usually spring-sown, although *bere* (winter barley) is known from other medieval accounts. Rye (*siligo*), a crop which fares well under poor conditions and on sandy and alluvial soils, is never mentioned in the Harmondsworth documents, presumably as the quality of the land and proximity to London markets, facilitating the ready sale of more valuable crops, made its cultivation unnecessary and uneconomic.

The Harmondsworth documents are full of references to the preparation of the demesne arable, the issuing of the seed-corn from the granary, sowing, hoeing, weeding and otherwise protecting and nurturing the crop, but it was during and immediately following the harvest, the climax of the farming year, that the barns became the centre of the manor's activities. The physical work was carried out by a variety of people. The demesne had a small, resident, paid labour force, which the accounts describe as the 'servants of the court' (*famuli curie*), who were put to work daily under the direction of the bailiff and other manorial officials. Their labour was supplemented at busy moments in the farming year by hired labourers, whose wages are recorded in the accounts and by the labour services of the customary tenants of the manor: the latter were usually deployed in specific tasks, such as hay-making or the harvest. The continued use of labour services, as revealed by the accounts of 1433–4 and 1450–1, was unusual, most lords having commuted them for money payments by this time, and was to be the cause of major unrest and labour difficulties by and after the mid-century (*see* p 58). One way or another, however, the whole population of the manor– men, women and children – must have been involved.

The surviving accounts all provide abundant details on the personnel and composition of the workforce at harvest time, and on their respective obligations, payment and feeding. For example, under the 'Expenses of the harvest' (*Custus Autumpnalis*) for 1433–4 (*see* Documents), are listed:

> For bread baked for the harvest – 5 quarters, 4 bushels of wheat at a price of 29s 4d. For ale brewed – 18 quarters of malt valued at £4 10s. For meat purchased for the harvest 5s beside 5 cows, 2 pigs and 3 geese ... valued at 40s. For salt fish purchased – 8s. For cheese, milk, butter eggs purchased for the harvest 18s. For onions amd garlic bought – 13d ... For three bushels of salt – 21d.

These provisions were for feeding assorted officers and tradesmen (a beadle, a carter, a swineherd , 'one brewer who is also the cook', one baker and two pitchers) 'being at the lord's table for five weeks this year'; the last three were also paid 6s 6d in cash. They also provided for two meals each for the manor's 77 customary tenants during that five-week period, specifically in return for the 'boon service' of reaping of 24 acres of barley, ie roughly one-third of an acre each. Meals for the duration of the harvest were also provided, it seems, for the manor's permanent menial staff, the *famuli*, perhaps twelve in number in that year, in line with the pairs of gloves provided (the account for 1450–1 suggests this more strongly);[319] these were owed in return for their work in reaping five acres of (unspecified) corn. The richness of the fare, perhaps especially the greater expenditure on meat than eggs, cheese and milk, is in keeping with the general national trend, apparent since the 1320s, for the quality of harvest food to increase.[320] The quantity of ale produced – at 60 gallons per quarter adding up to 1,080 gallons[321] – would also have been on the generous side, at over the standard

Fig 19
Illustration from the Luttrell Psalter (*c* 1320–40) showing the wheat harvest. The reapers are, as was usual for wheat, using sickles, grasping the stalks in the left hand and cutting with the right. The two reapers, not unusually, are women, as is the figure behind, standing up and stretching, and whose sickle appears to be lodged in her clothing. Behind, a man, sickle at his belt, binds a sheaf in readiness to take it to join the standing sheaf behind to form a stook. At his feet, ready to bind the sheaf is a 'bond', made of two handfuls of stalks knotted at the ear.
[BL Add MS 42130, fol 172v. Reproduced by kind permission of the British Library]

gallon a day per fed-day person (1,064), assuming that the *famuli* were fed for five weeks, and indeed further suggesting that they were: others, however, may have helped get through it, in addition to other ale brewed on the manor but not charged to the harvest. Meanwhile the inclusion of three geese in the bill – probably intended for an end of harvest feast or 'reapgoose' – and the plates, dishes, the '5 ells of cloth purchased to make a tablecloth' (in 1406–7),[322] and the 12lb of candles, also hint at an attention to decency and comfort, if the candles also imply long hours of work.

Much of the harvest work, however, was carried out by the same customary tenants, without cash or food payments, such as the

> 77 tasks of carrying corn provided by 38 virgators and 39 half-virgators each of whom having a cart shall carry 3 cartloads of corn from the field to the lord's barn receiving nothing for themselves nor for their horses. And those who shall not have a cart shall stack 3 cartloads of corn in the lord's barn.[323]

Hired labour was used too, however, as revealed in the cost of 'reaping, tying and carrying 101 acres of wheat, 66 acres of barley, 40 acres of pulse and 11 of oats' at £8 8s 9d, and the per-acre harvest costs calculated by the clerk at '10d, barley at 11d, pulse and oats at 10d' – the going rate for such work.[324]

Harvesting itself began with reaping the crop, in the case of wheat by grasping bunched stalks in one hand at knee height or higher (depending on its height), and cutting by drawing a sickle across them. Some sickles were serrated to make this easier. Other cereals were sometimes cut with a scythe,[325] necessarily therefore, closer to the ground. The cut stalks were then gathered and 'tied' – ie bound into sheaves with a straw 'bond'. These were then stooked, ie stacked in tipi-like cones (Fig 19 and *see* Fig 29), ears uppermost, and then, when sufficiently dried by sun and wind for a week or so, the sheaves were 'carried' in cartloads from the field to the barn doors (Fig 20). As the sheaves were delivered, the Harmondsworth granger may, as recommended in a number of treatises and presumably actually practised, have had a proportion of them (every 20th, 30th or 40th are recommended) immediately

Fig 20
The sheaved crop being carted from the field for storage. A man stands on the shaft at the front, driving the three horses uphill, and three more push from behind – one with a pitchfork, partly to prevent the sheaves from falling off, and another with his shoulder to the wheel. [BL Add MS 42130 fol 173v. Reproduced by kind permission of the British Library]

tus es fuperomnes deos

threshed (Figs 21 and 22), so as to provide an estimate for the eventual total yield of the harvest.[326] In any case, the sheaves were then stacked in the barn by 'stackers' (*tassatori* or *tassari*) – two of them in 1433 – working under the granger, and remained there until taken down for threshing. How much of the barn's interior was actually taken up by the crop is considered above, but filling it was, in any case, a skilled and arduous business, one 'stacker' pitching the sheaves up to another who laid them out in a stable fashion, pressing them down as he went. As the single demesne barn, the great barn must have been used to house different grains. No specific evidence of how this was arranged at Harmondsworth survives, but the practice is well attested elsewhere, including in the St Paul's accounts cited above: at Wickham St Paul (Essex), one barn was to be full 'of wheat (*frumentum*) from the entrance to toward the east, and from the entrance toward the west it must be full of oats. The centre bay opposite the entrance must remain empty';[327] at Walton (Essex), barn 'A', in about 1150, carefully delineated spaces were filled with stacks of barley, oats, wheat and rye (*siligo*).[328] A similar arrangement was recorded in the case of Wrington (Somerset), in 1189.[329]

Processing

Extraction from the stored crop 'in the ear' of the main product, ie grain, required the sheaves to be threshed and the raw product to be separated from the chaff, ie from the broken remains of the husk, the structural component of the ear. Similar methods were used to separate peas and beans, when dry, from their straw and pods.[330] These processes were as important, and, measured by man-hours, were more time-consuming than harvesting, and could account, at least as measured in later centuries, for a quarter of the work of a whole farm.[331] Extracting the grain was also integral to the function and the design of barns, as they provided the space to do it, for while warmer drier climates[332] allowed for outdoor threshing, in England it usually took place under cover.

How long the process took and how the work was programmed was subject to a number of factors. Threshing had to keep pace with demand for grain, but precedence had to be given to more urgent work, such as autumn and winter ploughing, safe in the knowledge that unthreshed grain actually improved in quality, at least for a year or so, as it continued to dry out. The process could therefore be extended into the spring. Then as now, different storage times also suited different grains, the 13th-century *Rules* requiring, for example, that oats were not to be threshed before Christmas.[333] Different crops also took different times to process, the longest being wheat, as remained the case when threshed mechanically: in the early 19th century, on the basis of systematically gathered and averaged figures, one man-day was required for every 5–6 bushels, but would produce 9–11 bushels of barley and 11–13 of oats;[334] the *Husbandry* applies a roughly similar norm, along with information related to other crops, in the late 13th century: 'And so one ought to thresh a quarter [eight bushels] of wheat and rye for two pence, a quarter of barley, beans and peas for 1½d, and one quarter of oats for 1d'.[335]

Threshing normally took place on the floor in the entrance bay (or bays) of the barn, sometimes called 'streys' (hence the misnomer 'threshing barn'): the surfacing of these floors could take many forms, and the absence of evidence for those at Harmondsworth in the 15th century is discussed above (*see* p 21). The streys were left clear when the barn was filled, and the sheaves thrown down on to them, starting with those at the top of the stacks in the adjacent bays. The exact practical details of what happened next, however, ie how the crop was actually threshed at Harmondsworth at the time of the barn's construction or at any other, is impossible to reconstruct in detail. For a start, the process varied according to period, crop type, available manpower and other practical factors. Moreover, generally speaking, threshing and related activity before mechanisation was so universal as to pass almost unobserved and unrecorded, but was so wholly obsolete in England by the mid-20th century as to be lost to memory: any attempt to describe and reconstruct this vital process therefore also relies on experimental archaeology, and contemporary parallels from elsewhere, especially eastern Europe.[336] These sources show that threshing could be done by individuals, pairs or gangs of men working together, as we can expect to have been the case at Harmondsworth, given the scale of the operation and the obligations on the customary tenants. The men used flails, of which no medieval English example survives, but which are depicted in numerous medieval illustrations, mostly of the 'labours of the seasons' type (Figs 21–2), and changed little into modern times:[337] they consisted of two heavy wooden rods, usually of ash, joined together by a hinge of hide, rope or iron; the thresher held the longer one – the four- or five-foot long 'handstaff' or 'helve' (modern terms), raised it above shoulder height, and brought the shorter but heavier 'beater' down flat upon the ear-end of the sheaves. A readily available film of the process held in the Néprajzi Múzeum archive, Budapest – and there must be others – shows a gang at work in the 1950s: four men thresh on the ground in front of the barn door, with the sheaves laid out in two rows of about 4m long, side by side and end to end, the men flailing roughly at right-angles to the axis of the sheaves;[338] numerous still photos from the same collection show further details and the construction of flails themselves. By way of an English (and indeed local) source, we may cite the rare description in John Middleton's *View of the Agriculture of Middlesex* of 1798. Following an account of the practice 'near London', whereby the threshers left the crop partly unthreshed so as to leave the straw more saleable, he tells us that

> they likewise strike perpendicularly, but incessantly without changing hands, or reducing the force of the blows, till the principal part of the corn be thrashed out on one side; they then turn the sheaf, and repeat the operation on the other side – they next change hands and strike in an oblique direction, which draws the straw from the sheaf an inch or two at every such blow, till the whole is completed. This gives them an opportunity of seeing and hitting every ear, till it be cleared of the grain.[339]

Different techniques and equipment, attested elsewhere from the 17th century, and above, were used if the straw was intended for thatching.[340]

Between batches the straw was picked up or raked away, leaving the grain on the floor, mixed with fragments of straw and chaff. This was then piled up nearby and the process repeated until a sufficient quantity had been accumulated for the grain to be winnowed, ie separated from the other debris. This was done by shovelling the mixture into the air while the winnower kept up a draught with a wicker winnowing 'basket' or fan, in a direction at right-angles to the shoveller's throw, across the suspended material, blowing away the chaff while the heavier grains fell to the ground.[341] Two such items (*vanni*) were bought for Harmondsworth for 2s in 1450.[342] In barns with opposing doors, on a breezy day a natural cross-draught could have helped the process, although the widespread idea that the door arrangement was necessary or even primarily intended for this purpose is nonsense: winnowing could perfectly well be done without them, as Harmondsworth and numerous other 'single-sided' barns demonstrate, and the main function of the 'opposing doors' was to allow carts to be driven into the barn for easier unloading and then driven through (rather than backed out), and to let in more light.

The threshers themselves were customary tenants undertaking this task as part of their labour services, the hired labourers (*famuli*), evident for example from the 1406–7 accounts, and which show that threshing and winnowing were done by taskwork (*ad tascham*) on a paid-for piece-work basis, thanks to the advantages that this brought to the employer.[343] Naturally, the fittest workers would be employed, as the work was notoriously arduous as well as difficult:[344] the *Seneschaucy* advises that ploughmen – necessarily, by modern standards, immensely fit and strong – 'ought to ... thresh'.[345] Several medieval treatises advise that the relatively light work of winnowing should be done by women and dairymaids in particular, thanks probably to their being the only regularly employed female farm workers and under-employed in winter.[346] Meanwhile, as always, the treatises advise on avoiding theft – the *Seneschaucy* advising that 'The reeve should take care that the threshers and winnowers do not take corn and carry it away in their dress, boots, shoes and pockets or in sacks and bags hidden near the barn'.[347]

On an operation on the scale at Harmondsworth, the whole thing was a formidable exercise. In 1406–7 the total quantity of grain expended (ie from the harvest of 1406) was 3,397 bushels and the equivalent in 1433–4, 3,167 bushels, which amounts to roughly 97 and 90 tons respectively.[348] At a rough estimate, based on an average of the man-days required for the main cereal types (at 9.166), threshing the harvest of 1406 would have taken 370 days and that of 1433, 345 – figures which exclude those of winnowing and other related tasks.

Accounting, use and distribution

Once the threshing and winnowing were complete, the grain was then transferred to the granary, from where, during the course of the remainder of the year and beyond, it was dispensed as required by the granary-keeper. According to the practice implied by the treatises and clearly the case at Harmondsworth, newly winnowed grain was measured in the barn under the granger's supervision by 'heaped bushel', ie we can assume, by over-filling the measure (a broad wooden, iron-bound cylinder), leaving a conical heap at the top: measurement itself was both necessary to quantify the crop, but also to pay hired threshers, or assess the notional cost, for accounting purposes, if they were customary tenants.[349]

The transactions between granger and granary-keeper were meticulously recorded with tallies, pieces of riven wood, usually ash, with notches cut into them recording significant units, and then split, so creating a duplicate record (as in an indenture) which defied forgery, as the two halves of the split stick marry up precisely or not at all. The granger had to preserve the stocks or main parts of the tallies because he had handed over the goods, that is the corn, while the granary-keeper kept the foils (the 'leaves') because he had taken charge of the corn.[350] A complexity arose, however, in that the granary-keeeper traditionally measured not by heaped but by levelled bushel, ie with the top of the measure levelled off with a straight stick, or (in early modern and 19th-century terminology, the strickle). As a result, a system had to be devised for ensuring that the quantity of grain issued by the granger matched, in fact and record, the quantity received and acknowledged by the granary-keeper, the difference being described in the treatises and the Harmondsworth accounts as the *incrementum*.[351] On this point the *Seneschaucy* sets out that

> No heaped measure ought to be taken from the barn into the granary to account for the 'increment' but with every eight quarters – in levelled measures – a ninth should be taken from the stackers for the 'increment', and no bushel, half bushel, or cantle should be handed over to the reeve [ie the granary keeper] from the threshers over and above the aforesaid measure.[352]

In other words, the actual quantities and number of bushels accounted for was matched by the granary-keeper by recording every eight heaped bushels received from the barn-keeper as nine according to his own, smaller 'stricken' measure. This practice is evident from the Harmondsworth accounts, although with slight variations according to grain type: with reference to the harvest of 1406, for example, wheat of various qualities 'issued of' the demesne and tithe barns amounted, according to the barn-keeper, to 1,145 heaped bushels, to which were added 71.5 bushels (71 bushels 4 pecks) to define the quantity, in his smaller units of levelled bushels, received and recorded by the granary-keeper: the ratio in this case being described as, and indeed adding up to, 'half a bushel from each quarter' – 1:16 (ie one-sixteenth was added to the granary-keeper's record of each bushel received from the barn-keeper). In the case of poor-quality wheat, the total quantity issued of both barns as recorded by the granger was 152 bushels, to which, for the purposes of the granary-keeper's (and so the final) account, was added 'for one quarter, one bushel and one peck from the heaping of the same, whereof a peck from each quarter',[353] ie a ratio or increment of 16:4. The accounts for 1433–4, in the first years of the Great Barn's use, are the same.[354] The treatises resound with warnings about the opportunities for fraud that this cumbersome system posed, all the more important at a time when even small quantities of grain were almost as negotiable as cash. At its most blatant the *Walter* warns that

> When corn is issued of thy barne have thou a faythful man that can charge the reeve in just manner for often tymes a man shal perceave that the barnekeeper and garneter doe ioyne together to doe falslye.[355]

Once in the granary, the grain was stored, presumably in timber bins. From there, it was dispensed for the purposes for which it was grown. These include payments (wages in kind), seed, animal food, malt (brewing) and sale. Thus, in 1433–4, taking these gross categories one by one, the cereal harvest of 1433, including tithes received in 1433, was consumed or disposed of as shown in Table 4.

These figures reveal a number of things. First, whereas landlords or institutions with large households, such as Winchester College, frequently took delivery of large quantities of grain and other products to feed them, this was not the case with the grain harvest at Harmondsworth, presumably because of its location: it has been variously calculated that overland transport costs for wheat in 1300 came to 2s 4d or 3s 5d per quarter for every ten miles,[356] which, over the approximately 75 miles to Winchester, would in the 1420s have added between one and two shillings per quarter. For the college, buying locally, or using the produce of more local manors, would therefore have been substantially more economic. The proportion used for seed, at 17.48 per cent rather less than the approximate one-quarter needed to

Table 4 Use of cereal crops of all types and pulses in the account for 1433–4 (harvested in 1433)

Use	Crop type	Quantities	Price	% of total crop (all types)
Payments	Wheat	457 bushels		11.35%
	Barley	16 bushels		
	TOTAL	**473 bushels**		
Seed	Wheat	264 bushels		17.48%
	Barley	320 bushels		
	Harascum	100 bushels		
	Oats	44 bushels		
	TOTAL	**728 bushels**		
Animal feed	Curallum	120 bushels		8.24%
	Barley	25 bushels		
	Harascum	84 bushels		
	Oats	114.5 bushels		
	TOTAL	**343.5 bushels**		
Feeding workforce	**TOTAL**	**204 bushels**		4.89%
Malt	**TOTAL**	**325 bushels**		7.80%
Sold	Wheat	824 bushels	680 bushels at 10d per bushel, ie £28. 144 bushels at 1s per bushel, ie £7 2s	50.21%
	Barley	960 bushels	1s per bushel, ie £48	
	Harascum	298 bushels	6d per bushel, ie £7 15s	
	Oats	9 bushels	3d per bushel, ie 2s 3d	
	TOTAL	**2091 bushels**		
TOTAL		**4164.5 bushels**	**£90 19s 3d**	

produce an equivalent harvest in the following year,[357] suggests that additional stocks were bought in from elsewhere, as was understood to be good practice at the time.[358] It is notable that the largest single proportion, at 50.21 per cent was that sold, of which 82.52 per cent was the most valuable, wheat. Total receipts from grain sales in 1433–4 came to £90 19s 3d, undoubtedly the largest single contributor to the gross cash revenue of the manor. Also notable is that in the case of wheat, the crop seems to have been sold in two batches, not of different grades (no *curallum* was sold), but presumably on separate occasions for different prices, probably made in the spring and then again in June and July; the later batches probably brought higher prices, although the phasing of sales was also related to the rate at which the crop could be threshed (*see* p 44–5), and the capacity of the purchasers to store it.[359]

In 1433–4 the grain was sold to a third party (*ut extra*). Who the buyer or buyers may have been, where the grain was eventually sold, how it might have got there, and what it was used for is worth some brief consideration. Harmondsworth, crucially, was at the very centre of the catchment for sale and consumption in London, an area of about 4,000 square miles, determined largely by transport costs and therefore very irregularly spread across the country.[360] In this context it is of interest that the proportion of barley sold was so large, influenced probably by the value of the uniquely enormous London brewing market, and perhaps that the manor sold so much wheat, of which the proportion sold to the London market was usually, because of its high value in proportion to transport costs, in inverse proportion to the distance.[361]

To serve this market, grain of all kinds could be bought directly from the manor, and carted off site at the buyer's expense,[362] but generally it would have been more advantageous for the manorial staff to arrange their own carriage for sale at the most appropriate local market, and on some manors – as in the case of Bec Hellouin's at Ruislip and Tooting – this duty was among those of the customary tenants.[363] In the case of Harmondsworth, the nearest grain market was Uxbridge, 6.5 miles to the north,[364] but given the meagre 17 miles to the capital, it seems more likely that the grain was taken directly, for sale, without intermediaries, to one or several of the major city cornmongers who supplied the city's vast demand.[365] If so, two main routes were available: overland to the Thames, for example at Richmond, and thence by boat to the city, or along the nearby 'Devils Highway', which passed Harmondsworth less than three miles to the south, entered the city at Newgate, and led immediately to one of the city's main corn markets, just inside.[366] Direct as the overland route would have been, economics, particularly as the Harmondsworth tenants had no duties to carry grain to market, point to the former: using Campbell's estimates of the cost of transporting a quarter of wheat ten miles overland at about 3s 5d and by river at about 3d, carrying the Harmondsworth crop overland to London would have cost about 7d per quarter, and by cart *and* river about 3s 5d (road leg) and by river 6d per quarter, and so 4s 1d, a significant difference even given any extra costs of transhipment and hire of boats and perhaps of carts.[367] The road leg of this journey would, according to the figures given by Campbell *et al*, have required 34 carts to carry the wheat crop alone, each pulled by three horses,[368] and accompanied by a carter. The boats were presumably hired, although some major Thameside landowners had their own.[369] The cornmongers' customers were bakers and brewers (among them some cornmongers themselves) and the 824 bushels of wheat were probably largely bought by the former for bread; the 960 bushels of barley would have gone partly for bread too, but mostly for malting;[370] *harascum* (298 bushels) could be used for bread, and the tiny quantity of oats (8 bushels) for animal fodder and brewing,[371] or conceivably bought for the horses used in carriage.

Grain, however, was not the only product of cereal farming, for straw was used for numerous purposes including thatching, fodder, animal bedding and an ingredient of compost, and this was taken directly from the barn for immediate use or stacked in ricks; its value was considered in the *Rules* to be 'worth as much of half the corn sold', and oat straw particularly so.[372] Straw too could be sold, although not at Harmondsworth, at least in 1433–4.[373]

Finally, it should be said that while the exercise of all these time-honoured processes and practices, year after year, may present an alluring picture of bucolic tranquility, by Wykeham's time Harmondsworth had had a long history of disastrous labour relations. The underlying problem had been the abbey's insistence on the performance of customary works, and their persistent refusal to allow their Harmondsworth tenants to commute their services, although they were willing enough when it came to their Ruislip tenantry.[374] This was exacerbated by the tenants' recurring claim, made as early as 1233[375] and with renewed vigour in 1276,[376] that the manor was 'ancient demesne of the crown', ie land that had been in royal hands in the reign of Edward the Confessor, on which rents and services were subsequently supposed to have remained constant; 1277 saw an open outbreak of violence, prompting the intervention of the constable of Windsor and the sheriff.[377] Trouble had flared up again a century later,[378] and there was, not surprisingly, an outbreak at Harmondsworth during the Peasants' Revolt of 1381, five men forfeiting their lands for rebellion.[379] At the time of Wykeham's acquisition, the tenantry were still regularly defaulting on their services, and the old problems were to reappear with a vengeance in the 1450s.

The Great Barn and its peers

In the case of barns, size matters. Claims abound for this or that barn to be the biggest in the county, the biggest in the country, 'the largest anywhere', both in popular and serious literature, in print and online.[380] The significance attached to individual barns can be closely bound up with size, sometimes with important consequences: in the case of Harmondsworth, its place in the national hierarchy, as then understood, formed a crucial part of the argument for English Heritage's purchase in 2011.[381] It therefore seems appropriate, in discussing a barn famed largely for its size, to identify that place as accurately as possible, and in doing so to assemble in one place, for the first time, the basic data on its rivals.

Any meaningful attempt needs to take account of known barns that no longer exist, and acknowledge that many have disappeared without trace, or remain to be discovered: the point is well illustrated by the complex of buildings belonging to Beaulieu Abbey discovered at Wyke, near Faringdon (Oxon) in the 1990s, which may include a barn as much as 80–90m long,[382] and the recent rediscovery of Abingdon Abbey's barn at Cumnor (Oxon), perhaps almost as large as Harmondsworth.[383] Other complications include post-medieval reduction in size, such as at Great Haseley (Oxon)[384] and Cumnor, or the enlargement of medieval barns, as for example at Patcham (East Sussex), where a five-bay barn of 1402–11 was extended by 10 bays c 1550 and by another four c 1610, giving it a total length of 76m (250ft).[385] Nevertheless, a number of lists have been attempted, some in size order, including that by Sir Henry Dryden in 1897 (which places Harmondsworth fourth),[386] Walter Horn's partial attempt of 1965,[387] and those by Mick Aston[388] and James Bond.[389] Attempts have also been made to classify barns by size – reminiscent of the oil-tanker categories 'Very Large' and 'Ultra Large' – most importantly by James Bond and John Weller and by Niall Brady: both identify categories of small, medium and large, the first classifying as 'large' buildings over 40m long × 9m (ie with a footprint of 360m^2), while Brady's threshold is set at a volume of 2000m^3;[390] in this category Brady has counted 23 examples among the 58 in southern Britain for which he had reliable dimensions.[391] With a footprint of 668m^2 and a gross volume of approximately 4,953m^3, Harmondsworth is very comfortably in the 'large' category by either reckoning, and as shown in Table 5, ranks no 13 among British medieval barns. It is not, however, among the group of three outstandingly enormous English barns at Minster, Cholsey (Fig 23) and Beaulieu (Fig 24), the smallest of which exceeded the area threshold for 'large' by nearly four times, and with footprints starting at 668m^2/7,200ft^2, might be termed 'Ultra Large'.

Unfavourable comparisons are sometimes made with medieval European barns, but only the astonishing building at Vaulerent (Seine et Oise, France; Fig 25) exceeds the English 'Ultra Large' examples in footprint. Among them, however, more than twelve can be shown to have been bigger than Harmondsworth, and many have a distinct architectural edge in the use of stone arcades,[392] unknown in

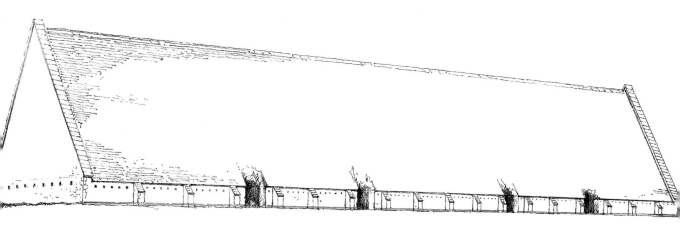

Fig 23
The great barn at Cholsey viewed
from the south-east in 1815, shortly
before its demolition, drawn by
J C Buckler. It was built for Reading
Abbey, probably in the 13th century.
The building was 303ft long and
54ft wide, the side walls about 8ft in
height; in plan it had a nave and two
aisles, 18 bays, with square stone
piers. In the early 19th century the
produce of the 1000-acre Manor
Farm filled this and two other
smaller barns.
[BL Add MS 36436, no. 681.
Reproduced by kind permission
of the British Library]

England, although Cholsey may have had stone piers.[393] Some are also architecturally
ambitious in other ways, with ornate gable ends (Ter Doest, Parçay-Meslay,
Fourcheret), carved capitals (Perrières,[394] Maubuisson) and other embellishments;
the barns at Ardenne, Maubuisson and Vaulerent also had built-in look-out posts at a
gable apex (in the latter two cases reached by spiral stairs).[395] Conversely, no French
barn appears to have contained a residential or 'office' chamber of the kind found at
Bredon and Great Coxwell, and which may have existed in the 13th century at Christ
Church Cathedral Priory's barns at Cheyham, Apuldre, Great Chert, and at the Sextry
Barn, Ely[396] (Table 6).

As the tables show, barns in England and on the Continent of and exceeding
the scale of Harmondsworth form something of a separate category. What, then,
might they share in origin and purpose, and what particular circumstances might
have led to their creation? The obvious common factor is that they were all created
by institutional or corporate owners, all ecclesiastical, and except for Harmondsworth
and Walton, all for the regular clergy.[397] This also, in fact, seems to have been the case
with the majority of barns of any real pretension at all: of the 288 medieval examples

Fig 24
The ruins of the great barn
at Beaulieu St Leonard's (Hants),
built for Beaulieu Abbey in the
first half of the 13th century. The
existing roofed barn was built
within the shell of the original
building, occupying about a quarter
of its footprint, after a fire in the
late Middle Ages.
[Photo David Robinson]

Table 5 The nineteen largest barns known to have been built in England in the Middle Ages: comparative data (measurements are all external)

Site	Builder	Form	Date	Dimensions	Footprint
Minster,[a] Kent TR 313 643	St Augustine's Abbey, Canterbury	Nave and (?) two aisles, stone walls. Destroyed c 1700.	Pre-Dissolution	352 × 47ft 107 × 14.3m	16,544ft² 1,530m²
Cholsey,[b] Oxfordshire SU 583 871	St Mary's Abbey, Reading	Nave and two aisles, 18 bays, stone walls and piers. Destroyed 1815.	14th century? Substantially rebuilt, 1430s[c]	303 × 54ft 92.35 × 16.5m	16,363ft² 1,523m²
Beaulieu St Leonard's, Hampshire SZ 406 983	St Mary's Abbey, Beaulieu	Nave and two aisles, 7 bays, stone walls, timber piers. Ruined by 16th century.	Early 13th century	224 × 67ft 68.27 × 20.42m	15,008ft² 1,388m²
Ely,[d] Cambridgeshire TL 538 802	Cathedral Priory of St Etheldreda, Ely	Nave and two aisles, 11 bays, stone walls. Destroyed 1842.	Mid-13th century	227ft 6in × 47ft 5in 69.35 × 14.47m	10,806ft² 1,003m²
Abbotsbury,[e] Dorset SY 577 850	St Peter's Abbey, Abbotsbury	Unaisled, 23 bays, stone walls, arch-braced roof (replaced, 11 bays roofless).	Mid-15th century	282 × 37ft 89 × 11.2m	10,434ft² 996.8m²
Chislet,[f] Kent TR 224 643	St Augustine's Abbey, Canterbury	Nave and two aisles, probably 13 bays.[g] Destroyed 1925.	12th and 13th centuries?	240ft long. Est 40ft wide 73.1 × 12.1m	9,600ft² 884m²
Waltham Abbey,[h] Essex TL 382 009	St Lawrence's Abbey, Waltham	Nave and two aisles, 12 bays (at fullest extent), timber framed. Destroyed c 1840. Excavated.	Two phases: 12th and 13th centuries	210 × 45ft 64 × 13.7m	9,450ft² 876m²
Walton,[i] Essex TM 252 220 (approx)	Canons of St Paul's Cathedral	Known only from 12th-century document.	Described 1142–68	168 × 53ft 51.2 × 16.15m	8,904ft² 826m²
Monknash,[j] Glamorgan ST 918 707	Abbey of Holy Trinity, Neath	Unaisled, stone walls, 11 bays. Roofless ruin.	13th century?	203ft 6in × 42ft 66.8 × 12.8m	8,547ft² 822.7m²
Littlebourne,[k] Kent TR 211 579	Cathedral Priory of St Andrew, Rochester	Nave and two aisles, 10 bays, missing 1.5 bays,[l] timber framed.	1307–27; roof, 1525[m]	202 × 39ft 61.6 × 11.9m	7,879ft² 733m²
Frindsbury,[n] Kent TQ 747 700	Cathedral Priory of St Andrew, Rochester	Nave and two aisles, 13 bays (3 destroyed), timber framed.	1404	218ft × 37ft 6in 66.7 × 10.75m[o]	8,248ft² 717m²
Tisbury,[p] Wiltshire ST 951 298	St Mary's Abbey, Shaftesbury	Unaisled, 13 bays, stone walls, raised crucks.	1289–1314	195ft 6in × 38ft 59.5 × 11.57m	7,429ft² 688.4m²
Harmondsworth, Middlesex TQ 056 777	Winchester College	Nave and two aisles, 12 bays, timber framed.	1425–7	192ft × 37ft 6in 58.52 × 11.42m	7,200ft² 668.29m²
Great Coxwell,[q] Oxfordshire SU 269 940	St Mary's Abbey, Beaulieu	Nave and two aisles, 7 bays, stone walled, timber arcades.	1292	152 × 44ft 46.32 × 13.41m	6,688ft² 621m²
Frocester,[r] Gloucestershire SO 786 029	St Peter's, Abbey, Gloucester	Unaisled, 13 bays, stone walls, raised crucks.	c 1300. Roof 16th century	192ft × 35ft 6in 58.52 × 10.82m	6,816ft² 613m²
Cumnor, Oxfordshire SP 461 041	St Mary's Abbey, Abingdon	Unaisled, 11 or 12 bays, stone walls, raised crucks.	14th century?	Up to 168ft 6in long × 36ft 6in 51.4 × 10.97m	6,588ft² 603m²
Bradford on Avon,[s] Wiltshire ST 823 604	St Mary's Abbey, Shaftesbury	Unaisled, 14 bays, stone walls, raised crucks.	Early 14th century	174ft 6in × 35ft 53 × 10.6m	6,017ft² 561.8m²
Hartpury,[t] Gloucestershire SO 779 236	St Peter's Abbey, Gloucester	Unaisled, 11 bays, stone walls, post-medieval roof.	14th century	161 × 36ft 49.07 × 10.97m	5,796ft² 538m²
Middle Littleton,[u] Worcestershire SP 080 471	St Mary's Abbey, Evesham	Unaisled, 11 bays, raised crucks.	From 1316	142ft 3in × 38ft 10in 43 × 11.88m	5,467ft² 510.84m²

a   Hasted 1797–1801, vol X (1800), 278: 'At a small distance from
    it [what] stood antiently a very large barn, sufficient to hold the
    corn growing on all the demesnes, being in length 352 feet, and in
    breadth 47 feet, and the height of the walls 12 feet, with a roof of
    chestnut. When the estate was divided, 154 feet in length of this
    building was carried to Sevenscore Farm, where it was burnt, by an
    accident unknown in 1700, and the remaining part here was burnt
    by lightning afterwards'. Presumably the buttressed south gable
    of the existing barn, aligned north–south, to the north of the court
    (observed by Edward Impey, 1980s) is a remnant of it.

b   Horn 1963; Hunt 1816. J Buckler's drawings (which must be in
    part reconstruction drawings) are at ML Add MS 36436, nos 680
    and 681.

c   Unpublished dendrochronological analysis (D H Miles, pers comm).

d   Willis 1843. The eastern end was at an angle, so Willis gives 'the
    mean length of the interior as 219ft 6in'. Its 'breadth between the
    walls' was 39ft 5in. The side walls were 4ft thick. The thickness
    of gable walls is not given but a plan (plate 11) indicates similar
    thickness. The volume could be calculated from Willis figs 4 and
    11. Side walls 12ft 8in high.

e   'Abbotsbury' in RCHME 1952, vol 1, 6–7; for the form of the
    original roof and approximate date, see Heaton 2007.

f   Rigold 1979, 34–35. Rigold's informant knew the barn when it
    was standing. He was unable to locate photographs or drawings.

g   Ibid, citing 1647 Parliamentary survey.

h   See Huggins 1972, 56–61; Hurst 1988, 895.

i   Horn and Born 1979, 365–9; Hale 1858, 130.

j   RCAHMW 1982, 262–6. The entry suggests no date but John
    Newman (1995, 45) notes that 'The most likely period for its
    construction would be the 13th c'.

k   See Austin 1997.

l   Ibid.

m   Arnold et al 2003.

n   Arnold et al 2002.

o   Measured on site by Edward Impey, 27 June 2012. Dimensions
    include the lost three bays (of which the sill walls survive).

p   For brief accounts see Andrews 1900, 30; Slocombe 2016. For
    the date, see Arnold and Howard 2016. The 1289–1314 date is
    the estimated felling date range. Measurements taken on site by
    Edward Impey.

q   See Horn and Born 1965; for date, see Munby 1988, 77 and Alcock
    and Tyers 2014, 123.

r   See Charles and Horn, 1983.

s   Andrews 1900, 27.

t   Visited by Edward Impey, 12 December 2014. On the date, see
    VCH, Gloucestershire, XIII, 87–8.

u   For the building see Charles and Horn 1966 and Andrews 1900,
    22. For the date, based on historical sources attributing the barn
    to Abbot John de Brokehampton, see Bond 1973, 16–18; for
    dendrochronology identifying a felling date after 1315, and thus
    that the barn was begun under Brokehampton but finished later,
    see Fletcher 1980, 34.

inventoried by Brady in southern England, only one even approached his 360m² threshold,[398] the raised-cruck building of 1342 at Winterbourne (Glos), which in its original 11-bay form,[399] at 339.3m², is in the 'large' category, but still 30 per cent smaller than that at Middle Littleton, the smallest comparator to Harmondsworth listed in Table 5. Of interest also is that of the total number of barns of any size in Brady's list, only approximately 90 (their status is not always known or given) were built for lay proprietors, hinting that the build quality and durability of small barns in ecclesiastical ownership may have been significantly better. Given that in the period between c 1300 and the Dissolution, the crown and lay landlords held roughly two-thirds of England's land, and enjoyed 71 per cent of its landed income as opposed to the 4 per cent drawn by the episcopacy and 25 per cent by collegiate and conventual proprietors,[400] both the comparative figures overall and the apparent monopoly of very large barns by the latter category of owner is very striking. Why might this have been the case? Part of the answer may be that the picture is distorted by a higher survival rate of institutional great barns, as seems to be the case with smaller ones, but the absence of any secular great barns suggests otherwise. More probable reasons for the disparity include the fact that ecclesiastical and institutional lords, generally speaking, tended to retain demesne farming longer and more extensively beyond its high point in c 1300 than secular ones, and so retained a more immediate motive (without the intermediary of a farmer), for capital investment in agricultural buildings. Another, which certainly helps explain the building of some of the largest examples, was that great ecclesiastical owners, particularly the older and greater Benedictine houses, held larger, more concentrated

Table 6 The twelve largest barns known to have been built in France and Flanders in the Middle Ages: comparative data (measurements are all external)

Site	Builder	Form	Date	Dimensions	Footprint
Vaulerent,[a] Seine et Oise	Abbey of Châalis	Nave and two aisles, 13 bays, stone walls and arcades, post-medieval roof.	1200–30	72 × 23m	1,656m²
Parçay-Meslay,[b] Indre-et-Loire	Abbey of Marmoutier	Nave, two aisles each side, 13 bays, stone walls, timber arcades. Roof burnt 1422 and rebuilt.	1210–27	60 × 25m	1,500m²
Allaertshuizen,[c] West Flanders	Abbey of Ten Duinen	Nave, two aisles, brick walls, 9 bays, stone walls, timber arcades. One gable partly survives.	1232–53	67 × 22m	1,474m²
Tranloy,[d] Oise	Abbey of Châalis	In original form, nave and two aisles, 10 bays, stone walls, timber arcades. Destroyed 1940.	Post-1205, pre 1426	c 70 × 20m	1,400m²
St Pierre-sur-Dives,[e] Calvados	Abbey of St Pierre	Nave, two aisles, stone walls, 13 bays, timber arcades. Rebuilt 1945.	1220–30	70 × 20m	1,400m²
Ten Bogaerde,[f] West Flanders	Abbey of Ten Duinen	Nave, two aisles, 10 bays, brick walls. Parts of gables and side walls survive.	1232–53	60 × 21m	1,386m²
Ter Doest,[g] West Flanders	Abbey of Ter Doest	Nave and two aisles, 9 bays, brick walls, timber arcades.	1370–85	56 × 22m	1,232m²
Stains,[h] Seine-et-Marne	Abbey of Châalis	Nave and two aisles, 12 bays, stone walls and arcades.	c 1200–50	56.8 × 21m	1,192m²
Maubuisson,[i] Val d'Oise	Abbey of Maubuisson	Nave and two aisles (one lost), 10 bays, stone walls, stone piers and arcade.	1240	47 × 21.8m	1,024m²
Fourcheret,[j] Oise	Abbey of Châalis	Nave and two aisles, 10 bays, stone walls, stone arcades. Two bays later medieval additions.	c 1206 and mid-13th century	19.6 × 52.20m	1,023m²
Troussures,[k] Oise	Abbey of Châalis	Nave and two aisles, 9 bays, stone walls, stone piers and arches. Ruined.	13th century	48 × 18m	864m²
Ardenne,[l] Calvados	Abbey of Ardenne	Nave and two aisles, 9 bays, stone walls, stone piers and arches.	Mid-13th century	48 × 16m	716m²

a   Horn 1968, 29; Blary 1989, 109–16
b   Chevalier 1995. Re dimensions, 588; re date, 589; date of destruction of original charpente 595, n23
c   Vincent Debonne, pers comm, June 2014
d   Blary 1989, 246–7
e   Epaud 2011, 194
f   Vincent Debonne, pers comm, June 2014
g   Horn and Born 1965, 33; dimensions from Nuytten 2005, 159 (plus wall thicknesses at 1m)
h   Blary 1989, 164–9
i   On the carpentry *see* Dietrich and Gaultier 2001; Kirk 1994, 91 fig 73; Hérard 1901
j   Blary 1989, 186–98
k   Blary 1989, 259–64
l   Chevrefils-Desbiolles 2007; for dating *see* Cazenave 1973, 72

arable-rich estates than most laymen, on which centralised and suitably equipped collection points would have made sense. Yet while this was the case for example with St Augustine's Domesday estate at Minster-in-Thanet (50 hides) and Abingdon's at Cumnor (30 hides), with proportionately extensive arable, Winchester's lands at Harmondsworth, or Beaulieu's at St Leonard's (for example) were not, by any yardstick, particularly large.

The best and simplest explanation for the comparative splendour of 'institutional' versus secular barns, however, probably lies in the confidence of perpetuity enjoyed by corporations, and their freedom from the vagaries of 'death, division, wardship and vacancy',[401] or vulnerability 'to asset stripping whenever the current incumbent died',[402] hardly incentives to invest in such buildings. Relative priorities, too, perhaps played a part: while secular owners were ready enough to spend vastly larger sums on great houses, for example, more than minimum investment in farmbuildings, however essential to their incomes, would have brought none of their immediate benefit to the comfort and prestige of the patron, or contributed to the conspicuous consumption which underpinned their status.[403]

Fig 25
The barn at Vaulerent (Seine-et-Oise). Interior view from the entrance end, looking north. Built for the Cistercians at Châalis in the early 13th century, the barn measures 72m by 23m, making it the largest of any known medieval barn in England or Europe. In common with many great barns in France, the aisle piers and arcades are of stone.
[Photo Yves Lescroart]

The barn and its environs, 1427–1543

Buildings and infrastructure

A certain amount is known about the development of the buildings at Harmondsworth after the construction of the Great Barn and while still in the college's ownership. The most important and best documented of these was another barn, known from the following entries in the bursars' account for 1434–5:

> In gift to a certain carpenter of Uxbridge for coming to the College in the same month for the making of a contract with the Warden for the building at Harmondsworth of a New Barn, 20d. For the expenses of John Godewyn for riding to Harmondsworth to seek the money that month beyond the expenses allocated to it in Roger Hubbard's bill, 4d. And for the expenses of Robert Vyport and others riding to Harmondsworth in the month of July with witnesses, having made a contract between the Warden and the carpenter for the making of one new barn there, 14s 6d. And in payment to John Lorimer for one horse hired for four days for Master Robert Vyport riding with the Warden at the same time, 16d.[404]

Until the first dendrochronological study was made of the Great Barn, it remained possible that it was the one mentioned in this account,[405] since when, of course, it has been clear that the barn of 1434–5 no longer exists. No source directly specifies the exact purpose of the later barn, but it seems likely that it replaced the building respectively called the 'corn barn' in 1397–8 and the 'tithe barn' in 1406–7, suggested above to have been one and the same. If so, it was also probably the 'Tythe barn', differentiated from the 'Great Barne' in 1598,[406] and very probably the 'Parsonage barne' mentioned in 1632.[407] Its site is not certain, but there are at least two indications that it extended eastwards from the south end of the Great Barn (ie at a right-angles to it, towards the churchyard). First, the hip of a large building in this position, complete with what appear to be vertically planked walls, and which is otherwise unaccounted for, appears in an engraving of 1796 (Fig 26).[408] Second, such a situation in relation to the Great Barn would fit the description in 1632 of the 'one barn', otherwise unnamed but reserved to Lettice, Lady Paget, 'standing and being at the northwest end of the parsonage barn'.[409]

In 1450–1 a series of general building repairs were accounted for, including thatching a stable and cow-house, and boarding the pigsty, while locks were bought for the brewhouse, the 'bailiff's door' and the pound. A few decades later attention turned to the manor house, which seems to have been wholly or at least partially rebuilt: the bursars' account for 1484–5 records that William Hill, accompanied by Robert 'the baker's boy', went to Harmondsworth to oversee 'various buildings being new made there at 3s 2d', and records the very substantial expenditure 'for the construction of the new buildings' of £41 18s 6d;[410] then in 1485–6 'repairs of new manor house at Harmondsworth' are recorded at 13s 4d.[411] The new work, in spite of later claims that it was demolished in 1774,[412] probably included the elaborate two-bay jettied structure depicted in pen and wash and pasted into the London Metropolitan Archives' grangerised copy of Daniel Lysons's *Environs of London* (Fig 27), dated 1794.[413] Drury has suggested that this was was an addition to, or partial rebuilding of, the pre-existing house.[414] The form of the building as depicted is compatible with the small-scale plan of the house on the 1816 map, suggesting that it survived until *c* 1820.

Fig 26
St Mary's church, viewed from the south-east. Engraving of 1796, based on an original by Samuel Lysons. Immediately to the left of the tower can be seen a vertical-boarded wall and hipped roof, probably belonging to the tithe barn of 1434–5, which stood until *c* 1800.
[LMA SC/GL/LYS no. k1247783. Reproduced by kind permission of the London Metropolitan Archive]

Fig 27
Pen and wash drawing of the Manor House at Harmondsworth dated 1794, probably by Samuel Lysons. It shows what is almost certainly the addition to the earlier house made in 1484–5, viewed from the east. The 15th-century work survived the partial demolition after 1687, but was replaced by the existing house *c* 1820.
[LMA, SC/GL/LYS No. k1248156. Reproduced by kind permission of the London Metropolitan Archive]

Events and economy

In about 1440 the warden and scholars successfully petitioned Henry VI that his purveyors should cease taking 'diverse maner of corn for your worthy household drawing to great value yn great hindrance' to the college, emphasising that Harmondsworth provided a 'grete part of the sustenance' of the community and its dependents.[415] A more difficult problem, arising once again from the tenantry's resentment of customary services, caused major disruption in the next decade. An arrangement made in 1446, whereby every tenant was to be granted the right to commute his harvest works for 2d per day, which should have done much to defuse the situation, clearly failed to take effect, or was perhaps rescinded:[416] indeed, in 1450 the college was faced with what amounted to a tenants' revolt,[417] subsequent legal expenses,[418] and extra labour costs 'because the customary tenants were unwilling to carry out their customary duties that year';[419] these included 33s for carting because the 'customary tenants refuse to carry this year'.[420] Quite possibly the tenantry was emboldened by the events of Jack Cade's rebellion in the summer of that year, although there is no evidence that Harmondsworth men participated, or of rebel activity nearby.[421] Formal commutation of most duties, however, was introduced in 1461, at the rate offered before, although some customary works were still being demanded into the 1470s.[422]

More radical than commutation, though, and no doubt partly prompted by these events, was the college's eventual abandonment of the long-cherished demesne system itself. The bursars' accounts for 1409–10 to 1411–12 (inclusive), and again in 1415–16 suggest an early flirtation with reform, as they name, in the place of *ballivus* or *serviens*, a *firmarius*, ie 'farmer' – William Tyghale (previously *serviens*), and then John Okebourne.[423] Taken at face value this would imply that the manor was indeed farmed in those years, although the choice of Tyghale as farmer suggests that, practically speaking, little had changed. In any case, the reappearance of a *serviens* from 1416–17, shows that this was a short-lived experiment.[424]

The first permanent adjustment in this respect was therefore that made in 1453–4, with the farming of the rectory, the revenues of which had previously been counted among those rendered annually by the bailiff: the farmer in question was one John Hardwell, paying £24 10s.[425] The crucial account, however, is that for 1456–7, which records the replacement of 'John Hubbard, bailiff' of previous years with 'Robert Iver, farmer' (*firmarius*), Hubbard now appearing as 'former bailiff', owing £8 6s 7d in arrears.[426] Hardwell, meanwhile, remained farmer of the rectory. Even then, however, the college's adoption of the system seems to have been a little cautious, as in that year and until the accounts run out in 1492–3, a new role appears – the 'collector of rents' (*collector*) who presumably brought in the rents of the non-demesne tenants, again formerly included in the bailiffs' returns and collected by the beadle. The Great Barn, meanwhile continued to serve its original purpose, although the tithe barn was now wholly at the disposal of the farmer of the rectory.

From 1492–3 until 1540 the accounts are missing, but by then the system of 'farming' of the manor had reached its logical conclusion, that is, the leasing of the entire estate and the rectory, excepting only the advowson, as a single lot in return for a fixed annual payment. The new tenants in that year were William Noke and his wife Joanna, who were to pay £50 a year for ten years and obliged to provide accommodation for college officials on their twice-yearly visitations. No reference is made to barns other than to the processes of storing crops and grain, but the usual provisions were made that all the 'houses and buildings of the manor' would be maintained.[427]

Winchester's own tenure, however, was nearing its close, for in 1543, the manor of Harmondsworth and the rectories of Harmondsworth, Heston, Hampton Isleworth, Twickenham and other property were taken by the king in exchange for other assets, all ex-monastic, scattered across Hampshire, Dorset and Wiltshire, and which included the sites of monasteries in Winchester itself and nearby.[428] As the annual value of the property given by the King exceeded what he received by £65, the college paid over an additional £1,314, ie 20 years' worth of the excess, to even the bargain.[429] Neither the reasons for the exchange nor the college's reactions are recorded, but the intention was not, as Kirby claimed, 'to enlarge the King's hunting ground at Hampton Court … called Hampton Court Chase',[430] which never extended north of the Thames.[431] The bargain lost the college its second most valuable estate, but was, at least on paper, not a bad one.

The barn and its environs, 1543–1987

Harmondsworth's second period of royal ownership ended in 1547 with Edward VI's grant of the lordship and manor to his father's former principal secretary, Sir William Paget,[432] appointed to a series of high offices in that year and made Baron Paget de Beaudesert in 1549.[433] Paget's descendants, barring a period of attainder between 1587 and 1597, held the manor until 1774, from 1714 as Earls of Uxbridge.[434]

In 1547, William Noke remained in place, but in 1587, on Thomas Lord Paget's attainder, the core of the manor was held of the king by Richard Tottle for £25 (in addition to Pery Place, held by copyhold at £8), and the rest by four other tenants. It was still noted that 'every customary tenant having a messuage or messuage platt and a plow must … carye in iiii loads of wheat or three loads of barley to the Lords Graunge', although the actual practice must have long since ceased. The 'howses' (ie buildings) of the manor were found to be in 'reasonable good repair'.[435]

By 1613 the manor was once again being managed as a single unit, leased for a year to Christopher Tyllier at £120, who had the right 'to have hold and enjoye the great barne that he now holdeth to lay in his croppe until the last day of May which shall be in the yeare of our Lorde God 1615.'[436] In 1632 the court lodge, ie the manor house, and all that went with it were leased to William King at £115 per annum, but the 'barn standing (ie the Great Barn) and being at the northwest end of the parsonage barne' was, puzzlingly, reserved to the Pagets.[437] The same rights were reserved again in 1662.[438]

Rents specified in leases of 1660, 1662, 1666 (2) and 1669 vary from £50 per annum to £160 per annum, implying very different packages of property, but in 1687 the Pagets' lease of Court Lodge to Joseph Pigg specified that he was to have 'two bayes in the Great Barne' at £50 per annum,[439] probably the arrangement under earlier leases which had applied strictly to the court lodge property in the most restricted sense. The other bays were presumably let to the other tenants or subtenants. The split use of the barn may have led to the insertion of partitions, as was certainly the case elsewhere, although the structural traces of this are inconclusive.[440] A new lease to Pigg, in 1698, added to 'so much [also] of another barne there commonly called the Great Barne', and 'The barne or building commonly called the tythe barne',[441] implying that he had thereby taken on the lease of the rectory too, and that the tithe barn was still in being: a lease to James Tillyer of the Harmondsworth tithes in 1738, in specifying its inclusion of 'that large edifice or barn called and commonly known by the name of the tithe barn in Harmondsworth', tells the same story.[442]

Meanwhile, in 1687 the landlord had also undertaken to take down

att his own cost and charges … and will with all convenient speed [to] alter the said mansion house by taking down all that left part of the said house from the entry by the hall and kitchen and the rooms adjoyning thereupon northward and westward.[443]

Clearly, given its depiction in the 18th century, all or part of the 15th-century work was left standing (*see* Fig 27) and the description suggests that it was the earlier hall and services of the house which were demolished, in keeping with Drury's suggestion that they were survivals from an earlier house, now obsolete and perhaps in poor repair.

In 1774 the manor was sold by the Pagets to John Powell Esq of Fulham, who was succeeded at his death in 1783 by his sister Elizabeth's eldest son, Arthur Annesley Roberts who took the name of Powell under the terms of his uncle's will.[444] His middle name hints at a connection – if probably of patronage not blood – with the descendants of Arthur Annesley, first Earl of Anglesey (cr 1661) whose title, raised to a marquisate, was bestowed on his Paget descendants in 1815.[445] It was probably in his ownership that the tithe barn of 1434–5 was removed, as it was depicted in 1796 but had gone by the surveying of the Enclosure map in 1816. Possibly, however, it was not destroyed but relocated, as in 1876 it was stated in James Thorne's *Handbook to the Environs of London* that the Great Barn had had a 'projecting wing at the N. end so as to form an L', and that this, 128ft long and 38ft wide and resembling the great barn in construction, had been taken down in the late 18th century and rebuilt at Heath Row.[446] By 'N', Thorne must have meant 'S', as he also places the tithe barn 'near the manor house', which he knew to have stood to the south of the Great Barn. That being the case, his story is plausible but not provable: in 1816 there was indeed a barn about 100ft in length called the 'Tithe Barn' on Braggs Lane, in the middle of the former Heath Row field,[447] still there although much altered in 1894,[448] but destroyed unrecorded by 1907 except 'for the great corner stones that … lie about the site'.[449]

Meanwhile, a series of multifoils or 'daisy-wheels' had been carefully compass-inscribed on several of the barn's Reigate stylobates, probably in the mid-18th to the mid-19th centuries, offering an interesting insight into the preoccupations of those whose livelihood was linked to the building. A good example can be found on the stylobate at truss 5, a more elaborate example adjacent to the door opening at truss 10 (*see* Fig 8), and there are others on the stone stylobates supporting the ends of the plates under the arcade posts. The only hexafoil inscribed on timber is on the south (door bay) face of truss 4, carefully inscribed on the tiebeam. Such marks have long been thought to have been apotropaic, intended to ward off witches, their familiars, bad luck brought on by the evil eye, and fire – a contention that has recently gained credibility through the work of Timothy Easton.[450] Typically these were placed adjacent to entrances, as is the case of Harmondsworth's hexafoils on truss 4, on the stone stylobate at truss 10, the stylobate of truss 7, and on the nave-facing side of stylobate at truss 11.

In Arthur Annesley Powell's time the functions of the Great Barn were recognisably those of the 15th century, and the farm, if anything, more concentrated than ever on cereals: as recorded in Peter Foot's *General View of the Agriculture of Middlesex* of 1794, Harmondsworth parish was 'entirely devoted to the purpose of the plough' and typically farmed on a rotation heavy in wheat, barley and oats;[451] wage-scales for threshing, now stood at 18d–20d per day.[452] While the acreage of

Fig 28

The interior of the barn, looking south, photographed in February 1887 by Percy Horace Gordon Powell-Cotton (1866–1940). In the foreground is one of the three threshing floors (bay 10), lit by the doorway to the left. The sacks and threshed straw suggest that threshing has recently taken place (probably mechanically). The far end appears to be stacked with sheaves awaiting threshing.

[Reproduced by kind permission of the Powell-Cotton Museum, Quex Park, Birchington]

arable, the produce of which the barn was used to store, was less than in the 1420s (the whole farm covered 205 acres in 1913),[453] and the work now done by paid labourers, the crops still grew in open fields and were harvested and processed by hand.

However, in the time of Arthur Annesley Powell's (d 1813) heir, his brother John Powell Powell (d 1849), the landscape of the parish was radically changed following the Enclosure Act of 1805,[454] and amending act of 1816,[455] finally enacted with the Enclosure Award of 1819,[456] which saw the enclosure of 1,100 acres of open and common fields and 1,170 of 'waste'.[457] Largely as a result, the arable area in the parish as a whole increased by nearly 100 per cent between 1800 and 1839.[458]

The barn's immediate environs changed too. The 15th-century house was finally demolished, some of its timbers being reused in a new stable, later salvaged during its remodelling in 1988–90 and now displayed in the barn.[459] The house was replaced in about 1820[460] by the existing yellow-brick building, just to the north-east of its precursor. A new timber-framed granary (relocated to its present site in the 1980s)

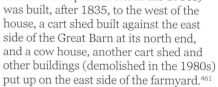

was built, after 1835, to the west of the house, a cart shed built against the east side of the Great Barn at its north end, and a cow house, another cart shed and other buildings (demolished in the 1980s) put up on the east side of the farmyard.[461]

At John Powell Powell's death in 1849 the property passed to his nephew, Henry Perry Cotton, son of his sister Harriot and her husband, Charles Bowland Cotton (later Powell-Cotton). The use of the barn itself was now also soon to change with the introduction of the threshing machine, the first functioning model of which had been produced in Scotland in the 1780s,[462] but which was relatively slow to catch on in southern England, unknown in Middlesex in 1798,[463] and as reported in Loudon's *Encyclopedia*, still rare in the county in 1828–31.[464] By the mid-century, however, and certainly by the 1880s, we can assume that wheat, at least, was being almost universally machine-threshed (Fig 28).

The Cottons – Henry Horace Powell Cotton from 1881 to 1894 and his son Percy Horace Gordon Powell-Cotton (1894–1940) – retained ownership of Manor Farm until shortly after the latter's death.[465] The tenants from 1824 until at least 1913 were the Hunts, at whose departure the lease was taken up by William Ashby,[466] whose family retained it, and from *c* 1940 owned it, until 1950. The middle decades of the 20th century were the last in which cereal crops were

grown in any quantity (Fig 29), in the 1940s filling about a quarter of the barn.[467] A little grain was still grown into the 1960s.[468] In 1950 the Ashbys sold 'Manor Farm' including the Manor House and 'the magnificent OLD TITHE BARN … in almost faultless order' and just over 45 acres through Knight, Frank and Rutley.[469] The buyer was Peter Purser, who sold the property to Mr Potter, the last farming owner, in 1978.[470]

The National Heritage Collection

The last link with farming of any scale or form was severed in 1986 with the sale of the barn, farmhouse and other buildings to John E Wiltshier Group plc, building contractors.[471] The company 'agreed the terms of a Section 52 agreement to spend £200,000 on making good the structure of the barn' and in 1988–9 substantial repairs were carried out to the sills, and props were inserted to the nave purlins.[472] In 1987, Listed Building Consent was given to remove added buildings. In 1991, substantial repairs were carried out, grant-aided to the tune of £30,000 by English Heritage (now Historic England).[473] An updated condition survey was commissioned by the London Borough of Hillingdon in September 2005.[474]

John E Wiltshier Group plc went into receivership in 2006, and the barn was offered to Hillingdon Council and English Heritage for £1.[475] Neither organisation, however, was willing to take it on, English Heritage's position being that the building was in reasonable condition and that viable economic use of the site was still possible. In the event the property was sold in more than one lot, leaving the barn surrounded by little more than its footprint, bought as a speculative venture by Harmondsworth Barn Ltd, registered in Gibraltar.[476] English Heritage's encouragement to maintain the building, offers of advice and grant-aid for repairs being of no avail, the building was added to English Heritage's Buildings at Risk Register in 2006.[477] In 2008 a series of urgent works necessary to put the building in a 'wind and watertight' condition were identified, but the owners refused to take action and by early 2009 it was obvious that English Heritage would need to take the initiative. In keeping with English Heritage's policy to reduce the number of dual designations (scheduling and listing), the building was de-scheduled on 19 October 2009,[478] which enabled the council to issue a formal Urgent Works Notice served on the owners on 11 November.[479] At a meeting with their agents on that day, it became clear that Harmondsworth Barn Ltd could not carry out the works and would go into receivership should cost recovery be attempted. The agents also indicated, however, that the company might be willing to offer the barn to a public body such as English Heritage 'for the nation'.[480] English Heritage was then in an unusual position, but the advantages of accepting the offer were very clear: first and foremost as the only realistic means of securing the future of a building for which any acceptable commercial use – thanks to the lack of scope for alteration, the constricted site and its situation – was highly unlikely, and to avoid the likely recurrence of the cycle of unsuccessful speculative purchase followed by neglect; second, the simultaneous opportunity to add the barn to the National Collection and make it publicly accessible. The third reason was financial: costs expended to date added up to £61,000 (legal fees and repairs), while serving a repairs notice and acquisition through compulsory purchase could have cost at least £50,000: while non-urgent but necessary repairs had been estimated at c £390,000, the reality was that English Heritage was the only source from which this would ever come. With the support of the Friends and of the MP John McDonnell a Business Case, including an assessment of the building's significance, was submitted to the DCMS on 8 August 2011[481] and agreed by the Secretary of State on 1 September 2011,[482] and the barn became the property of English Heritage on 17 October 2011.[483]

Preparations for an extensive repair programme were then put in hand, intended both to allow the building's removal from the Heritage At Risk Register and ensure its long-term stability. Following the usual preliminaries, Ptolemy Dean and Udo Heinrich of Ptolemy Dean Architects were appointed and Owlsworth & Co of Henley contracted to carry out the works, led on site by Dominic Barrington-Groves, reporting to Ndai Halisch, Project Manager, at English Heritage. Under their management and with the advice of other expert staff, the roof was re-battened with riven oak laths and covered with new hand-made tiles, the historic eaves overhang re-instated, repairs made to the timber frame, the original external boarding consolidated and new boarding fixed where it had been lost. Work began on site on the 7 April 2014 and was formally completed on 22 January 2015, at a total cost of £572,703.

The future management and maintenance of the site will be guided by the Conservation Management Plan commissioned from the Drury McPherson Partnership, completed in December 2014. Meanwhile the greatest single threat to the barn – its destruction by airport expansion – appears, at the time of writing, to have abated in part, but only in so far as Heathrow's expansion and the siting of its third runway, as recommended by the Final Report of the Airports Commission,[484] would at least leave it standing.[485] However, as the airport boundary would lie about 50m to the south and the runway about 150m, the immediate environment would be catastrophically degraded, the building threatened by vibration, and the amenity and public value of the site almost wholly lost. In the face of such threats, English Heritage and Historic England might need to consider whether leaving the building standing remained preferable to removal, an option deemed unacceptable 'if there was any viable alternative'.[486] At present, though, life goes on: the barn is open to the public, with the support of the Friends, on two Sundays a month in the summer, and information is offered to visitors through a variety of media.

Antiquarian interest, architectural legacy and early conservation interest

As with most supposedly 'vernacular' buildings, antiquarian and architectural interest in Harmondsworth was relatively late in coming: the earliest topographical works, Daniel Lysons's *Historical Account* (1800) and John Britton and Edward Brayley's *Beauties of England and Wales* (1816) both devote more space to the unremarkable church than to the Great Barn.[487] Lysons, though, did note the 'barn of remarkable dimensions, being 191 feet in length and 38 in breadth', and either he or his brother Samuel took the trouble to make a pen and wash drawing of the exterior (Fig 30).[488] Britton and Brayley's wording is almost identical.

Serious interest in the building and the origins of an important architectural legacy, however, began with the attention of no less a figure than Sir George Gilbert Scott (1811–78), who visited the barn in 1847 and made several sketches (Fig 31);[489] his then associate, George Edmund Street (1824–81) visited in the same year, perhaps on the same occasion, and produced a fine view of the interior.[490] Ten years later Scott cited Harmondsworth as a 'noble' example[491] among barns, and it may have been this one that triggered his enthusiasm for such buildings in general, prompting statements such as 'a Mediaeval barn is as good and true in its architecture as a cathedral',[492] long preceding William Morris's much-quoted description of Great Coxwell, in 1882, as 'the finest piece of architecture in England'.[493] More significantly, Scott also modelled his unbuilt scheme of 1850 for a church for Canterbury Settlement (later Christchurch) in New Zealand on Harmondsworth, if slightly elaborated.[494] In 1862, Scott again proposed a timber-framed aisled interior to the stone-shelled design for Christchurch cathedral, presciently citing its resistance to earthquake damage, which was accepted in 1862, but built only partly according to his plans and wholly in stone.[495] The New Zealand architect Benjamin Woolfield Mountfort (1825–98),

Fig 30
Pen and wash drawing of the barn from the south-east, made in 1792, probably by Samuel Lysons.
[London Metropolitan Archives, SC/GL/LYS no. k1248274]

Fig 31
Drawing by Sir Gilbert Scott
(1811–78) made on site in 1847.
Scott was very impressed by the
building and used it as a source for
several architectural commissions.
[RIBA SKB283/4]

possibly associated with Scott in his formative years (and certainly during the execution of his second design for Christchurch), may have been inspired at least by the scale of Harmondsworth in his designs of 1852 for Holy Trinity, Lyttleton.[496] Meanwhile, Scott's school dining hall at Bradfield College (Berks) had been completed in 1857, 'based on examples at Hillingdon and Harmondsworth',[497] and which certainly shares most major structural features with the latter.

At least one other major practitioner of the Gothic Revival, Basil Champneys (1874–1935) was similarly influenced: encouraged perhaps by his admiration of William of Wykeham (and his claims to be a collateral descendant), he built the library of Mansfield College (1887–9) in conscious homage to Harmondsworth, and its towering aisle posts and high arch-braced collars give an immediately reminiscent effect.[498] Not surprisingly, Harmondsworth also inspired at least one building of the Arts and Crafts movement, the Memorial Library at Bedales School (Hants), finished in 1922 to the designs of Ernest Gimson (1864–1919), who had visited the barn with W R Lethaby in the 1880s.[499]

The first published study of the building from an antiquarian perspective, however, was a two-page piece published in 1873 in the *Transactions of the London and Middlesex Archaeological Society*, by the antiquary Albert Hartshorne (1839–1910): as it happens, this initiative may also ultimately owe to Scott's interest in Harmondsworth, as Hartshorne was at least briefly one of his assistants or pupils,[500] and himself restored or embellished at least two Northamptonshire chancels in a Scott-derived style.[501] Hartshorne later wrote, in 1904, to T F Kirby, Winchester College's bursar and archivist, asking if he had any thoughts on the date of the building he had drawn and published decades before.[502] Hartshorne was also the first to raise concerns about the building's future, noting that 'one is almost afraid to think of it in connection with fire, to which, however, it will doubtless some day succumb',[503] as so nearly happened in 1972, and as has happened to so many others.[504] In the first decades of the next century, as the practical value of the barn diminished, the architectural historian Martin Briggs (1882–1977) noted in 1934 that 'It is most important that the Harmondsworth Barn, the finest in Middlesex, should be preserved'.[505] In 1937 the Royal Commission published their short account, probably by Alfred Clapham (1883–1950), with a photograph, plan and cross section, pronouncing its condition to be 'Good'.[506] Presumably prompted by their work, on 15 September 1936 the 'Barn at Manor Farm' was 'included in a list of monuments to be published' by the Commissioners of His Majesty's Works and Public Building (ie 'scheduled'). The typescript 'Short Description' on the official form notes that 'Mr Clapham considers that it may be 15th century ... It is in any case the finest barn in the County';[507] in March 1950 further official recognition was awarded with the building's listing in Grade I.[508] Meanwhile, the barn was being mentioned in numerous travel and topographical works, including by Arthur Mee, or his contributor, in his *Middlesex*, who on the eve of the Second World War, admired 'the "Gothic Barn", as it is called':[509] Pevsner described it in the 1951 *Middlesex* volume (the first of the *Buildings of England* series), as 'magnificent' and the 'seventh largest in the country', adding that it is 'one of the largest and finest aisled timber-framed barns in the country'.[510] Its best-known fan, however, was John Betjeman, who described it in 1973 as the 'the biggest and noblest medieval barn in the whole of England'.[511]

Documents

Transcribed by Stephen Priestley

Extract from the account of Robert Heate and Richard Boureman, bursars of Winchester College 29 Sep 3 Henry VI (1424) – 29 Sep 4 Henry VI (1425). WCM 22103, concerning the initiation of the building project. With translation.

Custus forin(sece) cum donis – In I virga panni empt(a) et dat(a) uxori Rogeri Huberd Ballivo de Hermondesworth xxiii d ob. Dato Johanni atte Oke iuxta Kyngston ad videndum meremium cum Willelmo Kyppyng pro grangia de Hermondesworth viii d. Item dato Willelmo Abbot de comitatu Middlesex pro labore suo in quadam materia concernante manerium de Harmond(sworth) de iiii acr(is) terre quas Johannes Jannes clamat tenere libere cum xii d dat(is) Johanni Gale venienti ad collegium in festo Sancte Thome Martir(i) iiii s iiii d.

Liberacio(nes) forin(sece) – In iiii^{ml} de bordnayll emp(tis) et miss(is) ad Dounton pro cancello ibidem cum xvii s i d ob pro xvii^{ml} de Lathenayll una cum iiii s viii d pro I^{ml} de Lednayll et CCC de Wat(er) nayll ultra vi li xiii s iiii d liberat(is) de stauro videlicet in plumbo empt(o) anno proximo preterito xxxix s iii d. In liberatio Willelmo Kyppyng carpentar(io) pro canc(ello) divers(is) fact(is) per eundem apud Donton per manus custod(is) vi li. Item in liberat(ione) Thome Waso carpentario pro rewardo et laboribus suis apud Alresford ultra convencionem suam ex gra(cia) custodis xxvi s viii d.
Summa – ix li v s xi d

Foreign expenses [lit. costs] with gifts – For one yard[512] of cloth bought and given to the wife of Roger Huberd bailiff of Harmondsworth 23½ d. In gift to John atte Oke near Kingston to view timber with William Kypping for the barn of Harmondsworth 8d. Also in gift to William Abbot of the county of Middlesex for his work in various matters concerning the manor of Harmondsworth of four acres of land which John Jannes claims to hold freely with 12d given to John Gale coming to the College on the feast of St Thomas the Martyr 4s 4d.

Foreign payments – For 4,000 boardnails bought and sent to Downton for the chancel there with 17s 1½d for 17,000 lathnails together with 3s 8d for 1,000 lead nails and 300 waternaylls ('waternails') over and above £6 13s 4d delivered from the store viz in lead purchased in the preceding year – 39s 3d. In payment to William Kypping carpenter for various works undertaken for the chancel by him at Downton by the hand of the Warden – £6. Also in payment to Thomas Waso [Vyse] carpenter as a reward and for his works at Alresford over and above his contract by grace of the Warden 26s 8d.

Total £9 5s 11d

Extract from the account of William Wyke and Richard Boureman, Bursars of Winchester College 29 September 5 Henry VI (1426) 29 September 6 Henry VI (1427). WCM 22104, concerning building costs. With translation.

Custus forins(ece) cum donis – In expensis domini Custodis et domini Johannis Edmond equitanc(ium) London ad loquend(um) cum Magistro Roberto Keton et ad supervidend(um) carpentar(ios) et tegulatores laborant(es) circa Grang(ia) de novo edificata apud Hermondesworth mense Augusti xii s ix d.

Liberac(iones) for(insece) – In CC di de Spykenayll CCC di de Ffyfstrokenayll vi Gosefett' vi Wodecobbeleez et xii gumphis pondera(ntibus) in toto CC lb precio lb ii d emp(tis) de Johanne Derfford Smyth et miss(is) ad Hermondesworth pro nova grang(ia) ibidem edificat(a) xxxvii s iiii d. In liberacione Rogero Houbard Ballivo ibidem iiii die Augusti in denar(iis) pro eadem grangia vi l. In dat(o)' Rogero Helyer ultra convencionem suam pro coopertura predicte grang(ie) xx s.

Foreign costs with gifts – for the expenses of the Lord Warden and Master John Edmond for riding from London to speak with Master Robert Keton and for supervising the carpenters and roofers working around the newly built barn at Harmondsworth in the month of August, 12s 9d.

Foreign payments – for 250 Spykenayll[s], 350 Fyfstrokenayll[s], 6 Gosefett 6 Wodecobbeleez and 12 hinge hooks[513] weighing in total 200lb bought at 2d per lb from John Derfford, blacksmith, and sent to Harmondsworth for the new barn built there, 37s 4d. In payment to Roger Hubbard the Bailiff there for the same barn, on the third day of August, in pennies, £6. In gift to Roger Helyer for the covering of the aforementioned barn, beyond his contract, 20s.

Extracts from NA SC6/1126/7, the account of Roger Hubbard Bailiff of Harmondsworth 29 Sep 12 Henry VI (1433 – 29 Sep 13 Henry VI (1434), concerning the cereal harvest. With translation.

Compotus Rogeri Hubbard ballivi ibidem a festo Sancti Michaelis anno regni regis Henrici VI xii usque idem festum (prox) anno predicti Regis xiii

Account of Roger Hubbard bailiff there from the feast of Michaelmas in the 12th year of the reign of King Henry VI to the same feast following in the 13th year of the said King.

Vendicio bladi – Et de xxxiii li ii s viii d de ciii quart(eriis) frumenti vend(itis) ut extra videlicet lxxxv quart(eria) prec(ium) quart(erii) vi s viii d. xviii quart prec(ium) quart(erii) v s iiii d. Et de xxxii li de cxx quart(eriis) ordei vend(itis) ut extra prec(ium) quart(erii) v s iiii d. Et de vii li ix s de xxxvii quart(eriis) ii buss(ellis) harac(ii) vend(itis) ut supra prec(ium) quart(erii) iiii s. Et de ii s iiii d ob de I quart(erio) I buss(ello) [et] di(midio) avene vend(itis) ut extra prec(ium) buss(elli) iii d. Et de xv s ix d de ii quart(eriis) v buss(ellis) braseii vend(itis) ut extra prec(ium) quart(erii) vi s.
Summa – lxxiii li ix s ix d ob.

Sale of grain – And [he answers] for £33 2s 8d for 103 quarters of wheat sold as beyond viz 85 quarters, the price of a quarter 6s 8d, 18 quarters, price of a quarter 5s 8d. And for £32 for 120 quarters of barley sold as beyond, at a price of 5s 8d a quarter. And for £7 9s for 37 quarters 2 bushels of pulse sold as above, at a price of 4s a quarter. And for 2s 4½ d for 1 quarter and 1½ bushels of oats sold as beyond, the price of a bushel 3d. And for 15s 9d for two quarters and 5 bushels of malt sold as beyond, the price of a quarter 6s. Total £73 9s 9½ d.

Custus Autumpn(alis) – In pane furnito pro expen(sis) Autumpn(alis) v quart(eriis) iiii buss(ellis) fr(umenti) prec(ium) xxix s iiii d [xxx s viii d crossed out]. In servis(io) bras(iato) xviii quart(eris) bras(eii) apprec(iatis) ad iiii li x s. In carn(is) empt(is) pro Autumpn(o) v s [ix.d crossed out] ultra v vacc(as) ii porc(os) et iii aucas de stauro apprec(iatas) ad xl s. In pissis sals(is) empt(is) viii s. In cac(eo) lacte butero et ovis empt(is) pro Autumpn(o) xviii.s [xix s viii d crossed out] In cepis et alleo empt(is) xiii d. In disc(is) et platell(is) empt(is) et in vasis ligneis sirculand(is) pro Autumpno xviii d. In xii paribus cirot(ecarum) empt(is) xviii d. In xii lib(ris) candel(arum) empt(is) xviii d. In iii buss(ellis) sal(is) empt(is) xxi d. In bruera falcan(da) contra Autumpn(um) xii d. Et tam expend(itis) hoc anno que I budell(us) I carect(arius) I porcar(ius) I brasiat(or) que simul est cocus I pistor et ii tassat(ories) exist(enti) ad mensam domini per v septimanas hoc anno et lxxvii custum(arii) metent(i) blada ad ii precar(ias) exist(enti) ad mensam domini ad ii repast(os) sunt in eisdem expens(iis) que messor ligan(dis) et comportan(dis) ad ii precar(ias) xxiiii acr(arium) ordei. In bladis metend(is) per famulos Curie v acr(e). In ci acr(is) frumenti lvi acr(is) ordeo xl acr(is) haras et xi acr(is) avene metend(is) ligand(is) et comportand(is) viii li viii s ix d et sic est messio cuiuslibet acr(e) frumenti ad x d ordei xi d haras et avene ad x d. In stipend(iis) ii tass(atorum) in Autumpno xiii s iiii d. In stipend(iis) I coci et I pistor(is) xiii s iiii d.
Summa xi li xix s ix d.

Expense of the Harvest – For bread baked for the Harvest – 5 quarters, 4 bushels of wheat at a price of 29s 4d. For ale brewed – 18 quarters of malt valued at £4 10s. For meat purchased for Autumn 5s besides 5 cows, 2 pigs and 3 geese in store valued at 40s. For salted fish purchased – 8s. For cheese, milk, butter and eggs purchased for Autumn – 18s. For onions and garlic bought – 13d. For dishes and plates purchased and for hooping wooden barrels for the Harvest – 18d. For 12 pairs of gloves bought – 18d. For 12lbs of candles bought – 18d. For 3 bushels of salt purchased – 21d. For mowing heath land before the Harvest – 12d. And expended this year for 1 beadle, 1 carter, one swineherd, one brewer who is also the cook, 1 baker and 2 pitchers being at the lord's table for 5 weeks this year and 77 customary tenants reaping the corn for two customary services, being at the lord's table for two meals during the same Harvest for reaping, tying and carrying for two customary services – 24 acres of barley. For reaping corn by the servants of the Court 5 acres. For reaping, tying and carrying 101 acres of wheat, 66 acres of barley, 40 acres of pulse and 11 acres of oats – £8 8s 9d, and thus is the service for each acre of corn at 10d, barley at 11d, pulse and oats at 10d. For the wages of 2 pitchers at the Harvest – 13s 4d. For the wages of 1 cook and 1 baker – 13s 4d. Total – £11 19s 9d.

Frumentum – Rogerus Hubard ballivus ibidem respond(et) de cxi quart(eriis) iiii buss(ellis) de exitu grangie dominice mens(uratis) et trit(uratis) ad thascam et vannat(is) per tall(iam) contra Willelmum Appulby contratalliat(orem). Et de lxvi quart(eriis) iiii buss(ellis) peiorum de eodem exitu trit(uratis) et vann(atis) per tall(iam) ut supra. Et de v quart(eriis) iiii buss(ellis) de cumul(o) eorundem quorum videlicet de quolibet quarterio pec(ia). Et de xiiii quart(eriis)

Wheat – Roger Hubbard bailiff there answers for 111 quarters 4 bushels of the issue of the demesne barn measured and threshed at taskwork and winnowed by tally against William Appulby the controller. And for 66 quarters 4 bushels of poor [wheat] of the same issue threshed and winnowed by tally as above. And for 5 quarters 4 bushels of the heaping of the same viz from each quarter a peck. And for 14 quarters of best-quality wheat of the issue of the tithe

melior(is) frumenti de exitu grangie decim(arum) trit(uratis) et
vannat(is) ut supra. Et de iiii quart(eriis) I buss(ellum) peiorum
frument(orum) de eodem exitu trit(uratis) et vannat(is) per talliam ut
supra quo videlicet de quolibet quarterio pec(ia).
Summa ccii quarter(ia) ii buss(ella).

De quibus in semine super cvi acr(as) terre in divers(is) furlong(is)
super acram ii buss(ella) [et] di(midium) – xxxiii (rest defaced) ...
liberacione ballivi per annum vi quart(eria) iiii buss(ella) cap(iente)
per septimanam I buss(ellum). In liberacione I bedell(i) [rest defaced]
I carect(and) I daie que simul est firmare lactag(ii) et vacc(arum)
iii caruc(atorum) iii fugat(orum) et I porcar(ii) per annum L I
quart(eria) vii buss(ella) quolibet cap(iente) quart(erium) ad x
septim(anas). In convenc(ione) seminator(is) semenis I buss(ellum).
In convencione fabri fabrici ferrament(um) iii caru(carum) per annum
iii buss(ella). In pane furnato [text missing] expen(sis) Autumpn(alis)
v quart(eria). In convencione Willelmi Appulby contratall(iatoris)
ii buss(ella). In dono domini [text missing] et cuidam de Curia (?)
domini Regis I quart(erium) ii buss(ella). In vendicione infra ciii
quart(eria). Et super comp(otum) ii buss(ella) [et] pec(ia).
Summa que supra. Et eque.

Curallum – Et de xiii quart(eris) curall(um) de exitu frumenti grangie
dominice trit(uratis) et vannat(is) per talliam ut supra. Et de exitu
frumenti grangie decim(arum) trit(uratis) et vannat(is) per talliam
ut supra.
Summa – xv quart(eria).

Et totum comp(utat) in dato et prebendo equorum – Et eque.

Ordeum – Et de clvi quart(eriis) I buss(ello) ordei de toto exitu
grangie dominice trit(uratis) et vannat(is) per tall(iam) contra
Willelmum Appulby contratall(iatorem). Et de xxii quart(eriis) vi
buss(ellis) de toto exitu grangie decim(arum) trit(uratis) et vannat(is)
per tall(iam) ut supra. Et de v quart(eriis) iiii buss(ellis) de cumul(o)
eorundem quorum videlicet de quolibet quarterio pec(ia). Et de iii
quarter(iis) on(eratis) super comp(otum).
Summa clxxxvii quart(eria) iii buss(ella) [et] di(midium).

De quibus in semine super lxxx acras terre in divers(is) furlong(is)
super acram iiii buss(ella) - xl quart(eria). In convencione Appulby
contratall(iatoris) I quart(erium). In convenc(ione) seminator(is)
I buss(ellum). In dato porc(is) et porcell(is) iii quart(eria) I
buss(ellum). In vendicione infra cxx quart(eria). In brasio inferius
fuso xx quarter(ia). Et super comp(otum) iii quart(eria) ii buss(ella)
[et] di(midium) per xvii s viii d.
Summa que supra. Et eque.

grange threshed and winnowed as above. And for 4 quarters I bushel
of poor-quality wheat of the same issue threshed and winnowed by
tally as above viz from each quarter a peck.
Total 202 quarters 2 bushels.

*Whereof in sowing upon 106 acres of land in various furlongs,
2½ bushels on an acre – 33 [quarters] ... in payment of the bailiff
per annum 6 quarters 4 bushels, receiving 1 bushel a week. In
payment of the beadle ... 1 carter, one dairy maid who is both the
keeper of the milking and the cows, three ploughmen, three drivers
and one swineherd per annum – 51 quarters 7 bushels each
receiving one quarter for 10 weeks. And by agreement with the
sower of seeds – 1 bushel. And by agreement with the smith making
the ironwork of 3 carts – 3 bushels per annum. For bread baked for
the harvest – 5 quarters. In agreement with William Appleby the
controller – 2 bushels. In gift to the lord ... and to a certain person
of the lord King's court – 1 quarter 2 bushels. Sold (as within) 103
quarters. And upon this account – 2 bushels & 1 peck.
Total as above. And equal.*

*Curallum – And for 13 quarters of curallum (inferior quality wheat)
of the issue of wheat of the demesne barn threshed and winnowed by
tally as above. And for the issue of wheat of the tithe barn threshed
and winnowed by tally as above.
Total – 15 quarters.*

*And he accounts for the whole given for the provisioning of horses.
And equal.*

*Barley – And [he answers] for 166 quarters 1 bushel of barley of
the total issue of the demesne barn threshed and winnowed by tally
against William Appulby the controller. And for 22 quarters 6 bushels
of the total issue of the tithe barn threshed and winnowed by tally
as above. And for 5 quarters 4 bushels of the heaping viz for each
quarter one peck. And for 3 quarters charged upon this account.
Total – 187 quarters 3½ bushels.*

*Whereof in sowing upon 80 acres in various furlongs, 4 bushels on
an acre – 40 quarters. And by agreement with [William] Appulby the
controller – 1 quarter. In agreement to the sower 1 bushel. In feeding
the pigs and piglets 3 quarters one bushel. In sale 120 quarters. For
inferior quality malt brewed – 20 quarters. And upon this account
3 quarters 2½ bushels for 17s 8d.
Total as above – And equal.*

Haras(ium) – Et de xlviii quart(eriis) vi buss(ellis) haras(ii) de exitu amb(arum) grangie trit(uratis) et vann(atis) per tall(iam) ut supra. Et de x quart(eriis) de eodem exitu per estimacionem in silignis. Et de I quart(erio) iiii buss(ellis) de cumulo eorundem videlicet de quolibet quarterio pec(ia)
Summa lx quart(eria) ii buss(ella).

De quibus in semine super xl acras terre in divers(is) furlong(is) super acram ii buss(ella) di(midium) xii quart(eria) iiii buss(ella). In dato columbell(is) in yeme iiii buss(ella). In dato equis et porc(is) per estimacionem in silignis x quart(eria). In vend(icione) infra xxxvii quart(eria) ii buss(ella).
Summa que supra. Et eque.

Avene – Et de xx quart(eriis) I buss(ello) avene de toto exitu ambarum grang(ie) trit(uratis) et vannat(is) per tall(iam) ut supra. Et de v buss(ellis) de cumul(o) eorundem quorum videlicet de quolibet quarterio pec(ia).
Summa – xx quart(eria) vi buss(ella).

De quibus in semine super xi acr(as) in divers(is) furlong(is) super acram iiii buss(ella) – v quart(eria) iiii buss(ella). In prebendo equorum de Custod(is) venient(is) ibidem trium vice hoc anno, videlicet xx die Aprilis, primo die Junii et vi die Junii per iii bull(as) sigillat(as) vii buss(ella) [et] di(midum). In prebendo equorum Domini Custodis existenti ibidem dum idem fuit London bina vice ii quart(eria) ii buss(ella). In prebendo equorum Domini Ricardi Beryman et Johannis Godwyn veniend(is) ibidem in negoc(iis) Domini per I bull(am) sigill(atam) I buss(ellum). In prebendo equorum Senescalli clerici et aliorum veniend(is) pro cur(ia) tenenda et aliis negoc(iis) faciend(is) vi buss(ella). In prebendo equorum vicecomitis Middx ad turnos Sancti Marci et Hock(day) I quarter(ium). In prebendo equorum herciand(um) ad utriusque semen – iiii buss(ella). In farina facta pro potagio famulorum et pro expens(iis) autumpni v quart(eria). In vend(icione) infra I quarter(ium) I buss(ellum) [et] di(midium). Et super comp(otum) ii quart(eria) pro iiii.s.
Summa que supra. Et eque.

Brasium – Et de xx quarter(iis) ordei recept(is) supra pro braseo inde fuso. Et de v buss(ellis) de inc(remento) mensur(e) et factur(e) videlicet de quolibet quarterio pec(ia).
Summa - xx quart(eria) v buss(ella).

De quibus in servisia brasiata pro expens(is) Autumpni xviii quart(eria). In vendic(ione) infra ii quart(eria) v buss(ella).
Summa que supra - Et eque

Pulse – And for 48 quarters, 6 bushels of pulse of the issue of both barns threshed and winnowed by tally as above. And for 10 quarters from the same issue by estimate in dry sheaves. And for 1 quarter 4 bushels from the heaping of the same viz from each quarter 1 peck. Total – 60 quarters 2 bushels.

Whereof in sowing upon 40 acres of land in various furlongs, 2½ bushels on an acre – 12 quarters 4 bushels. Given to the doves in winter – 4 bushels. Given to horses and pigs by estimate in dry sheaves – 10 quarters. Sold (as within) – 37 quarters, 2 bushels. Total as above. And equal.

Oats – And for 20 quarters 1 bushel of oats of the issue of both barns threshed and winnowed by tally as above. And for 5 bushels from the heaping of the same, viz a peck from each quarter. Total – 20 quarters 6 bushels.

Whereof in sowing upon 11 acres in various furlongs, 4 bushels on an acre – 5 quarters 4 bushels. For feeding the horses of the Warden coming there on 3 occasions this year, viz on 20th April, 1st June and 6th June by 3 sealed letter – 7½ bushels. For the feeding of the horses of the lord Warden being there while he was in London on two occasions – 2 quarters 2 bushels. For the feeding of the horses of Sir Richard Beryman and John Godwyn coming there on the lord's business by one sealed letter – 1 bushel. For the feeding of the horses of the Seneschal, clerk and others coming there to hold courts and undertake other business – 6 bushels. For the feeding of the horses of the Sheriff of Middlesex for two 'tourns' [held on] the feast of St Mark and Hockday – 1 quarter. For the feeding of the harrowing horses at both sowings – 4 bushels. For meal made for the servants' pottage and for harvest – 5 quarters. Sold (as within) 1 quarter, 1½ bushels. And upon this account – 2 quarters for 4s.
Total as above. And equal.

Malt – And for 20 quarters of barley received for brewing malt. And for 5 bushels from the increase of the [heaped] measure and the making [thereof], viz one peck from each quarter. Total – 20 quarters 5 bushels.

Whereof in ale brewed for the Harvest – 18 quarters. Sold (as within) – 2 quarters, 5 bushels.
Total as above. And equal.

Notes

1 Jenkins 1993, 66–7. Oft-repeated claims that Betjeman 'dubbed it the Cathedral of Middlesex' seem to be untrue.

2 Ibid.

3 The abbey was founded under Duke Robert II, dedicated to the Holy Trinity, and given the suffix in the charters 'de monte Rothomagi' (Deville, 1840, 421–3; Pommeraye 1662, 4–6), the 'mons' being the hill that still bears that name to the south-east of the medieval city. From its foundation, however, the monastery possessed relics of St Catherine, and was later (as implied by Pommeraye 1662, 24–5, from the late 12th or early 13th century) more commonly known by this dedication, or as, in the title of his work 'dite de Ste Catherine'. See also Decaëns 2003, 20.

4 £20,000 is approximately a skilled carpenter's annual take-home wage today. The annual wage of a carpenter in the early 15th century was about £5 per year. If the cost of the barn was approximately £90 (see pp 16–17) at 15th-century prices, it would have allowed for the employment of 18 carpenters for a year. For context see Dyer 2002, 240.

5 The figure includes VAT at 20 per cent and excludes further sums which may be spent on the external boarding. Ndai Halisch and Lyndsay Summerfield, English Heritage, pers comm, January 2015.

6 Drury McPherson Partnership 2014.

7 Bond and Weller 1991, 57–8.

8 Munby and Steane 1995; Dyer 1997; Higounet 1965; Blary 1989.

9 Brady 1996.

10 The known version of the text adds that 'Haec donatio facta est per unum cultellum, quem prefatus rex joculariter dans [sic] abbati quasi eius palmae minatus infigere: "Ita, inquit, terra dari debet"' (This grant was made by means of a small knife which the aforesaid Duke jokingly gave to the abbot as if he were going to stab him in the palm, saying "This is the way land should be given"), Deville 1840, 455, no. LXVII. The grant was made at the royal manor of Gueritho, that is, King's Worthy (Hants), not (pace Bates 1988, no. 232) at Winchester. On the legal and procedural context etc, see Tabuteau 1988, 119–35.

11 See most importantly Matthew 1962, 26–71.

12 Impey 2004, 432; Timson 1973, vol I, 207–9, no. 325.

13 'terram quae anglice Hermodesodes nuncupatur, cum ecclesia et omnibus sibi pertinentibus, scilicet in agris, pratis, pascuis, molendinis, aquis, humectis, silvis, ceterisque huiusmodi eidem villae contiguis', Deville 1840, 455, no. LXVII.

14 Middlesex 6.1.

15 No property of the abbey is mentioned in Domesday, but a confirmation charter of the Conqueror records the gift: 'Arnulphi de Hesdin in Middlesexia manerium quod vocatur Ruysslep totum, excepta i hida que iam data erat sancte Trinitati de Monte'. (of Ernulf de Hesdin the whole manor of Ruislip, in Middlesex, except for one hide now granted to Holy Trinity of the Mount.) Salter 1925, 73–5. The VCH Middlesex (IV, 135) concludes (surely wrongly given omission in Domesday?) that the gift had been made in 1069.

16 Middlesex 10.1.

17 VCH Bucks I, 212; Farrer and Clay, 1914–65, vol 3, 176; Hudson Turner 1847.

18 VCH Bucks, IV, 249–50; VCH Middlesex, IV, 7.

19 VCH Middlesex, I, 200; Blomefield 1805–10, vol 2, 519.

20 VCH Middlesex, I, 200. The medieval St Leonard's church, on the site later occupied by the now destroyed Methodist church, was destroyed in the early 15th century. The site is now within the bounds of the 19th-century settlement of St Leonards-by-Sea. Manwaring Baines 1986, 113.

21 VCH Middlesex, I, 201.

22 VCH Middlesex citing E 106/2/1.

23 VCH Middlesex, IV, 7.

24 VCH Middlesex I, 201; Shipp 2008, 242; Cal Pat Rolls Richard II, vol IV, AD 1388–92, 378.

25 See p 12.

26 NA SC12/11/20; SC11/444. The document has so far been attributed to the early 12th century (VCH Middlesex, II, 66–9), but in reality can be dated on the basis that it was drawn up in the time of Abbot Robert and Prior William Burden: Robert was in office from 1231 and Burden moved on to become Prior of Blyth in 1273 (VCH Nottinghamshire, II, 88; Pommeraye 1662, 29–31.

27 'Item abbas sive prior debet prepositum et preconem de suis hominibus ad voluntatem suam et quieti erunt de toto redditu et alio servicio suo prepositus manducabit cotidie ad mensam domini vel habebit qualibet ebdomadem unum boisellum frumenti'. (Also the abbot or the prior shall have a reeve (prepositus) and a preco from among his men at his bidding, and they will be free of all rents and other services, and his reeve shall eat daily at the lord's table or he shall have every week a bushel of grain.) (NA SC12/11/20; SC11/444, clause 54). Preco is not a term found elsewhere in the Winchester material examined in the course of this study, but is given as a synonym for serviens (normally translated as 'serjeant' or 'reeve'), in DuCange and Heschel 1840–50, vol 6, col 453c; Howlett et al 2009, 2387, gives 'beadle, sergeant or similar official'.

28 NA SC6/1126/5.

29 WCM 11501.

30 NA SC6/1126/6.

31 Davis 2007, *passim*; Shipp 2008, *passim*.

32 Davis 2007, 146–7.

33 Davis 2007, 143; Evans and Faith 1992, 644.

34 Davis 2007, 143–4, 149–50; Shipp 2008, 185.

35 Morgan 1941–2, 206; Shipp 2008, 188–90; Matthew 1962, 117.

36 Wykeham had obtained permission in 1385 to buy secular properties up to the value of £100 (Shipp 2008, 163–4, citing WCM 700).

37 Shipp 2008, 189; Davis 2007, 150; Evans and Faith 1992, 644.

38 Shipp 2008, 189–90; Evans and Faith 1992, 646.

39 Evans and Faith 1992, 646; Matthew 1962, 116.

40 Davis 2007, 150–3; Evans and Faith 1992, 646–8; Shipp 2008, 282–3.

41 Kirby 1903, 344.

42 For the text, *see* Kirby 1903, 344: 'comme il appartient a avoir aus Religieux de leur estat'. For the implication that the monks may have stayed in England but not at Blyth, *see* Matthew 1962, 117.

43 *Cal Pat Rolls*, Richard II, vol IV, AD 1388–92, 434.

44 WCM 11382; Shipp 2008, 242.

45 Shipp 2088, 242.

46 WCM 22077 (riding expenses for initiating the work and viewing quarry works and carpentry) and WCM 22080a (dedication by the Bishop of London).

47 Kirby 1902, 345–6.

48 Shipp 2008, 242.

49 Christopher Dyer, pers comm.

50 The values of St Leonard's by Hastings, Saham Toney and Tingewick in 1291 – a figure available to buyer and seller – were respectively £2, £2 and £22. Adding these to the annual value of 80 marks p.a. (£53 6s 8d) in 1392 arrives at £79 6s 8d, ie *c* 27 years' revenues; if the Harmondsworth Farm figure of £80 paid by the monks from 1338–69

(*see* p 2) is used, the total is £106, ie almost exactly one-twentieth of £2,150.

51 Shipp 2008, 238.

52 *Cal Pat Rolls* Richard II, vol IV 1388–92, 417–18. Or, as put in the licence by Richard II to the Abbot and Convent of St Catherine's to grant to Wykeham the manor of Harmondsworth and other estates on 10 March 1391 (WCM 11376) the college received at Harmondsworth the '*manerium de Hermondesworth cum pertinentiis et advocacionem et patronatum dicte ecclesie de Hermondesworth cum pertinentiis et advocacionem ecclesie de Hermondesworth cum advocacione vicarie eiusdem ecclesie terras tenementa boscos redditus servicia et possessiones supradicta in dicto comitatu Mddx*'.

53 LMA/4455/009. On the date of the map, *see* Wild 2006, 27.

54 *VCH Middlesex*, IV, 1. The water-courses have a complex history and have been subject to changes (ibid, 2).

55 Ibid.

56 Phillpotts 2010, 7–9.

57 For the suggestion that Southcote was identical to or superseded by Heath Row, *see* Phillpotts 2010, 19–20.

58 Sherwood 2009, 65–7.

59 NA SC12/11/20 (attached to custumal; *see* note 26): '*Et sunt in dicta parochia xxxviii virg(atarii) terre et xxxix semivirgatarii et xlv cotar(ii)*'.

60 London Metropolitan Archive AC0446/ EM 1 (undated late 14th-century rental). The calculation assumes a Virgate of 30 acres. The *VCH*'s dating of the document to the early 15th century is incorrect (*VCH Middlesex*, IV, 10, n55) as the text refers to the 'land of the convent of St Catherine's'. Stephen Priestley, pers comm.

61 I am grateful to Mark Bailey for advice on this point.

62 Gies and Gies 2002, 124–5, offer a simple explanation: 'Where three fields were used, one lay fallow all year, a second was planted in the autumn with winter wheat or other grain, the third

was planted in the spring with barley, oats, peas, beans, and other spring crops. The next year the plantings were rotated. In the two-field system one field was left fallow and the other divided in two, one half devoted to autumn and the other to spring crops. In effect, the two-field system was a three-field system with more fallow, and offered no apparent disadvantage as long as enough total arable was available.'

63 Phillpotts 2010, 14–15.

64 Hillingdon Archives, Map 543; *see also VCH Middlesex*, IV, 4.

65 *VCH Middlesex*, IV, 4.

66 *VCH Middlesex*, IV, 3–4, and map on p 5.

67 Wild 2006, 27.

68 For example, WCM 11502: '*cx acras iacentis in diversis quarentenis*' (110 acres lying in various furlongs').

69 NA SC12/11/20.

70 WCM 11503.

71 LMA, AC0446/EM 1.

72 WCM 10744.

73 I am grateful to advice from C J Bond on this point.

74 NA SC12/11/20 and SC11/444, clause 48: '*Tenentes abbatis apud Ryslepp debent harietum redempcionem terre pasuagium et sectam ad curiam sicut homines de Harmond*'. (The abbot's tenants at Ruislip owe a heriot for the redemption of the land, pannage and attend the court just as the men of Harmondsworth.)

75 *VCH Middlesex*, IV, 135.

76 *Cal Pat Rolls* Edward VI, vol I, AD 1547–8, p 45.

77 *VCH Middlesex*, IV, 136.

78 Impey 1991, II, 9, fig 3.

79 WCM 78; WCM 70b.

80 WCM 70b; WCM 78; Shipp 2008, 236. The buildings at St Cross had been those of a small priory of the abbey of Holy Trinity, Tiron (Eure-et-Loir).

81 WCM 70a: '*graves et intollerabiles expensas quas in edificacionibus ecclesiarum capellarum grangiarum domorum et aliorum operium …*'

a tempore fundacionis annuatim sustinuimus'.

82   WCM 78. The chancel was dedicated in 1396–7 (WCM 22080a). Total rebuilding is inferred by payments concerning both quarrying and carpentry in 1394–5 (WCM 22078).

83   Harvey 1978, 135, 277.

84   WCM 78.

85   RCHME 1937, 60–1. The window tracery dates from 1862–3 (*VCH Middlesex*, IV, 19), but follows its form: *see* Lysons 1800, plate opp. p 136.

86   NA E101/2/1; NA E106/7/18 no. 9; NA C145/139 no. 19; WCM 10744; NA C270/17 no. 7.

87   WCM 70b: '*et camera nova ibidem'.*

88   WCM 11502; *see also* Kirby 1903, 350–1.

89   WCM 11502; NA E 106/7/18 no. 8; NA C270/17 no. 7.

90   NA SC6/1126/6.

91   On the last point, *see* Dyer 1994, 87.

92   NA C145/139 no. 19.

93   WCM 10744.

94   WCM 11501 ('*domos domini*').

95   WCM 11503.

96   NA SC6/1126/6.

97   WCM 11503: '*In stipendiis ii carpentarii prosternentum i quercum in gardino et scapulancium eandem pro i stayre ad ostium granarii*'. On the Bradford-on-Avon granary *see* Bond 2004, 139–40. When required, such buildings could clearly be vast and elaborate, such as the Great Granary at Norwich Cathedral Priory (Slavin 2012, 135–40).

98   NA C145/139 no. 19; WCM 10744.

99   WCM 11503.

100 Ibid.

101 Assuming a total cultivated area of 2,260 acres and demesne arable, including fallow, at 470 acres.

102 Drury McPherson Partnership 2014, 25; Pathy-Barker 1989; Cowie 2014.

103 The earliest dated barn in England is the Barley Barn at Cressing Temple (Essex): *see* Tyers 1993; Fletcher *et al* 1985, 41 (Barley Barn, soon after 1220; Wheat Barn, about 60 years after Barley Barn; Granary, after 1575); Tyers 1990, 45–6 (Barley Barn, 1200–40; Wheat Barn 1257–90; Granary 1409); Tyers and Hibberd 1993 (Barley Barn 1205–30; Wheat Barn 1257–80); Tyers *et al* 1997 (Wheat Barn, 1417–43 (later phase); Granary, 1412/13 (later phase)).

104 Hale 1858, 130; Horn and Born 1979, 366–9.

105 On Perrières, *see* De Caumont 1846–59, IV, 619–22. The roof was destroyed by fire in December 2013. The barn at Austrebosc (Commune of Coudray-en-Vexin) was damaged in the storm of 1987; the surviving carpentry, later demolished, was seen by the author shortly after and roughly dated (with advice from Yves and Elisabeth Lescroart) by its use of lap-dovetails. On the possible connection with Marmoutier: Charpillon 1868, I, 863.

106 Commune of Rouvillers. For the (dendrochonological) dating, *see* the Dendrotech database (www.dendrotech.fr/frDendrabase/site), consulted August 2015. I am grateful to M Jannick Ledigol for advice on this point.

107 I am grateful to M François Blary for advice on this point.

108 WCM 11335.

109 NA SC12/1/20.

110 NA SC6/1126/5.

111 NA E 106/7/18 no. 8 (Extent); NA SC6/1126/5 (Account).

112 NA SC6/1126/6 '*et pro quadam p(er)annell p(ar)iet(is) grangie lathand(a) iiid*'. I am grateful to Stephen Priestley for advice on this point.

113 *In ii carpent(ariis) conduct(is) ad emendand(um) tign(um) portice grangie frumenti groundsull(andis) et stodand(is) ii spacia eiusdem grangie ad tascham iii.s iiii d. In vi mill(enis) d tegul(is) plan(is) empt(is) ad idem xxxvii s ix d. In quart(erio) buss(elli) calce petre empto ad idem ii s. In dict(is) tegul(is) et calce car(iantis) de Harefeld usque Harmond' per carect(as) domini iiii vicibus xii d. In iiii buss(ellis) aven(e) emp(tis) pro preben(do) equorum xx d. In dcc*

lacchez emp(tis) ad idem iii s vi d tam pro dict(a) portic(a) quam pro parva dom(o) iuxta granar(iam) lacchand(is). In v mill(enis) lacchenail emp(tis) ad idem v s x d prec(ia) millene xiii d. In ccl hopetiell(s) gotertiell(s) et ryggetiell(s) emp(tis) pro goteris dicte portice tecta eiusdem et tecta predicte parve domus … In conv(encione) I cooperator(is) cooperient(i) super predict(am) porticam … necnon divers(as) defectus super magnam grangiam magno vento peiorat(am) ad tascham xxvi s iii d … In I coopertore conducto ad cooperiendum super magnam grangiam cum stramine per ii dies xii d.

114 Unless the hip-tiles were for the porch.

115 Torching might seem unlikely in a barn, given the importance of ventilation, but note that in 1358–9, 20 quarters of lime were bought 'for tiling' the new barn at Gamlinghay, Cambs, in addition to the purchase of the tiles themselves (Rackham 1993, 9; also Sherlock 1991, 13).

116 As for example at the granges of Norwich Cathedral Priory (Slavin 2012, 120), or at Walton on the Naze (Essex): Horn and Born 1979, 366–9; Hale 1858, 130–1 (re Walton on the Naze) and 135 (re Ardeley, Herts).

117 I am grateful to Mrs P M Ryan for confirmation that the names of these barns probably pre-date the 20th century. For other examples, *see* Steer 1950, which identifies nine farms with both 'wheat barns' and 'barley barns', and others for peas, oats and hay; at the home farm of Evesham Abbey, a barn built between 1324 and 1327 was said to be specifically for barley (Bond 1973, 13).

118 WCM 11503.

119 On hay barns, *see* Brady 1996, 9.

120 WCM 11503.

121 Ibid. For example, the 148 quarters of barley were issued from the lord's barn and 56 from the tithe barn.

122 WCM 11502.

123 Ibid.

124 WCM 11503.

125 WCM 11502: a roofer was paid for covering '*parvum domum iuxta granariam et murum prefix necnon diversas defectus super magnam grangiam*'.

126 WCM 11503: '*I murum tren* [sic] perhaps derived from *transversum? ab Angulo grangie dominice usque ad sepem gardini quod continetur iiii perticatas at v pedes*'.

127 Drury McPherson Partnership 2014, 24–5.

128 SC 2/191/22.

129 LMA Acc0446/ED/152 (lease of Court Lodge, 20 February 1632); LMA, Acc0446/ED/156 (lease of Court Lodge, 1 June 1662).

130 WCM 11503.

131 *VCH Middlesex*, II ('Ancient Earthworks' (1–14)), 6; Mowl 1988, 18; RCHME 1937, 61.

132 *VCH Middlesex*, II ('Ancient Earthworks').

133 Sherlock 1991, 13.

134 As the Drury McPherson Partnership 2014, points out (p 25).

135 I am grateful to Christopher Dyer for advice on this point.

136 WCM 22078, 22079, 22080, 22082, 11502, 22084, 22085 and 22099, 22100, 22313, 22101, 22102, 22314, 22103.

137 WCM 22880, 22315.

138 Wood-Jones 1956, 43 and plate C.

139 *See* p 40.

140 WCM 22103 and WCM 22108.

141 Kirby 1892, 184–90. On the circumstances and decision-making processes surrounding the building of the Great Barn at Bredon in the 1340s, *see* Dyer 1997, 26.

142 Peas were stored in ricks at Harmondsworth in 1388–9 (NA SC/1126/6), and on the Worcester Cathedral Priory estates (Christopher Dyer, pers comm), Hale 1858, 130 (at Walton on the Naze).

143 I am grateful to Toby Murphy and Andy Crispe of Historic England for providing these figures.

144 Weller 1986 12, section 3.3; Brady 1996, 62.

145 Hale 1858, 130 (Walton on the Naze, Essex).

146 As in the case of the barn at Wrington (Somerset) in 1189: *see* Stacy 2001, 185–6.

147 Weller 1986, 12, section 3.e; cites manorial account for Chastleton, Oxon, of *c* 1330s: '*i meya usque ad magna trabes frumenti et siliginis mixti*' (one mixed stack of wheat and rye up to the tie beams); this was the case at Ardeley and Thorp (Hale 1858, 131). On the Latin terminology for the fabric, interiors and loading of barns, *see* Weller 1986, drawings at p 38.

148 Weller 1986, 12, section 3.d., citing Osney Abbey's accounts for Aldsworth (Glos): '*due meye drageti excedentes altitudinem murorum*' (two stacks of dredge rising above the height of the walls), and (ibid) re Bibury (Oxon), another Osney manor, '*In magna grangia … est i meia frumenti excedens altitudinem murorum*' (in the great barn … is one stack of wheat rising above the height of the walls).

149 As at Wrington in 1189 (Stacy 2001, 185–6). This was probably a cruck or raised-cruck building.

150 Hale 1858, 130, re Walton on the Naze: behind the stack previously described, the barn '*plena est usque ad festum*'; Stacy 2001, 185–6; Dyer 2015, 86.

151 John Weller's conclusion, based partly on the St Paul's accounts, was that 'storage capacity does not (normally) equate with volume, but only up to the *trabes* and the barn may be filled from end to end or space may be left for threshing. Subject to further data, I suspect that once a barn has a wagon passage, the latter is unlikely to be filled with sheaves (except in a flush crop) and accounts which show a full barn may indicate one without a wagon passage' (1986, 12, section 3.e).

152 Dyer 2015, 88; Dyer 2012, 321.

153 '*Ad estimacione grangie. Memorandum quod una meya frumenti in grangia est latitudinis xxx pedum in uno spacio inter duo furcos longitudine xv pedum et altitudine parietum x pedum continebit communiter xl quarteria*'.

154 I am grateful to Christopher Dyer for this information. The stacks measured 8 × 13 × 5ft (2.43 × 3.96 × 1.52m) and 8 × 8 × 6ft (2.43 × 2.43 × 1.82m), ie 520ft^3 (14.62m^3) and 384ft^3 (10.74m^3), giving in-sheaf volumes per quarter of 173ft^3 and 128ft^3, averaging at 150ft^3 (4.22m^3).

155 Weller 1986, 10–11.

156 Stephen Letch, pers comm, 12 May 2013.

157 Oschinsky 1971, 275: 'In August the bailiff should … command … that the bundles and sheaves are small; the corn will then dry quicker, one can load, stack and thresh the smaller sheaves better and there is more wastage in large sheaves than in small ones'.

158 Brady 1996, 157; Brady 1997, 93.

159 NA SC6/1126/7.

160 WCM 11503; NA SC6/1126/7.

161 Higounet 1965, 63–4.

162 WCM 22103.

163 WCM 22104.

164 Ibid.

165 Dominic Barrington-Groves, pers comm.

166 WCM 11503 (1407).

167 WCM 22316 and 22104.

168 WCM 22316: '*cancellatur [super] Rotulum Bursariorum*'. I am grateful to Malcolm Mercer and Stephen Priestley for advice as to the meaning of this note.

169 WCM 22104, m1: '*Hermondesworth – Et de Rogero ballivo ibidem nichil hoc anno quia totum ad edificac(ionem) nov(e) grang(ie) ibidem*'.

170 WCM 22315, WCM 22105.

171 WCM 78; Shipp 2008, 236.

172 Titow 1969, 203–4. The extract from the Account Roll is given in translation.

173 Thompson 1998, 103–4, 108.

174 WCM 78; Shipp 2008, 236.

175 Rackham 1993.

176 Dyer 2002.

177 Christopher Dyer's estimate of the cost of the 9-bay Great Barn at Bredon

in *c* 1340 at 'near to £50', ie £5 10s per bay or 22d per m², if applied to Harmondsworth produces figures of £66 and £61 (Dyer 1997, 26).

178 Titow 1969, 204.

179 Brady 1996, 149 and n13, 383–4; Munby and Steane 1995, 341–3.

180 WCM 78.

181 Mark Bailey, pers comm, June 2014; Harvey 1987, 170.

182 Harvey 1987, 170.

183 The chancel proper has a 19th-century roof replacing a 14th-century one (RCHME 1987, 130) and the north transept one of 16th-century appearance; the account wrongly attributes both transept roofs to the 17th century (p 131). The south transept roof has arch-braced tiebeam trusses with short king post and ridge beam with two struts either side and short posts under chamfered purlins.

184 J Morrin, pers comm, citing WCM 3090, draft text for *VCH Hants,* ns II *Mapledurwell,* from which this information was omitted.

185 Gee 1952, 118.

186 Ibid, 165.

187 Munby and Steane 1995, 346.

188 WCM 22084.

189 Harvey 1987, 257.

190 For example, Davis 2007, 131.

191 WCM 22104.

192 'Ultra convencionem suam pro coopertura predicte grangie xx s': Account of William Wyke and Richard Boureman, Bursars of Winchester College 29 September 5 Henry VI (1426) – 29 September 6 Henry VI (1427) WCM 22104, m4. See the almost identical wording in the 1424–5 Bursars' accounts relating to Thomas Wyse's work at Alresford, for which he was awarded '*ultra convencionem suam ex gracia custodis 26s 8d*' (over and above the contracted price by the kindness of the warden, 26s 8d). (WCM 22103).

193 Account of William Wyke and Richard Boureman, Bursars of Winchester College 29 September 5 Henry VI

(1426) – 29 September 6 Henry VI (1427), WCM 22103.

194 Tyers and Hibberd 1993. Earlier scientific dating attempts had included both radiocarbon (Berger 1970, 45–6, 125), which placed the barn at the 'turn of the thirteenth–fourteenth century', and (inconclusive) dendrochronology by and based on fieldwork by Veronika Siebenlist with Walter Horn and Freddie Charles in the 1960s; their sampling sites were noted by Tyers in 2012: *see also* Tyers 2015, 1.

195 Tyers 2015, 5.

196 Miles 2005.

197 Paul Drury's observation.

198 Robinson and Worssam 1989, 595–600.

199 WCM 78. For plan see RCHME 1937, 60.

200 Robinson and Worssam 1989, 598.

201 The flint nodules are unworn and must have come directly from a chalk quarry, of which the nearest could have been in the Chalfont to Rickmansworth area 8 to 10 miles (13–16km) to the north (B Worssam, pers comm, July 2012).

202 Not Totternhoe as previously described (eg Hartshorne 1873, 418); Bernard Worssam, pers comm 6 July 2012.

203 I am grateful to Tim Easton for advice on this point.

204 Drury McPherson Partnership 2014, 36, citing Thompson *et al* 1988, 82.

205 Hartshorne 1873, 417–18, interior view and plan.

206 Munby and Steane 1995, 361–3.

207 *See,* for example, Brown 1794, 52, where the author describes a method of laying such a floor.

208 Hardy, *Far From the Madding Crowd,* 127. The Weatherbury barn is supposedly based on the gigantic medieval barn at Abbotsbury in Dorset (Harper 1904, 237). *See also* Fig 28.

209 Slavin 2012, 121. Slavin interprets this as a 'storey', not a practical arrangement in a barn, or at least in one used for storing sheaves.

210 *See,* for example, Munby and Steane 1995, 353.

211 The barn was thoroughly studied in 1990 by Peter McCurdy who produced an extensive series of measured drawings at ½-inch-to-1-foot scale. These drawings are meticulously detailed and show every shake, peg, assembly mark and nail. They also show all areas of decay and structural deficiencies together with proposals for repairs in an accompanying document. These documents have been used extensively by the present authors in studying the building. More recently (2012) a detailed study and detailed photographic record of the building was carried out by the HAWK Institut Baudenkmalpflege (Kohnert 2012), led by Dr Tillman Kohnert.

212 Tyers 2015, 5–6. The dating was based on the analysis of five offcuts retained by Peter McCurdy in the 1980s, three of which produced dates.

213 Drury McPherson Partnership 2014, 40, item 2.8.19.

214 Salzman 1952, 244.

215 Paul Drury's observation (Drury McPherson Partnership 2014, 40).

216 *CC di(midium) de Spykenayll CCC di(midium) de Ffyfestrokenayll, vi gosefett, vi Wodecobbeleez et xii gumphis ponderantibus in toto CC lb preci(um) lb ii d emptis de Johanne Derfford Smyth et miss(is) ad Hermondesworth pro nova grang(ia) ibidem edificat(a) xxxvii s iiii d.* (250 Spykenaylls, 350 Ffyfestroknaylls, 6 gosefett, 6 Wodecobbeleez and 12 hinges, weighing in total 20 lb at 2d per lb bought from John Derfford, smith, and sent to Harmondsworth for the new barn built there, 27s 4d.) (WCM 22104).

217 Salzman 1952, 304–6.

218 Ibid, 315.

219 Each common rafter has one nail, and the principal aisle rafters have two. Nine common rafters per bay × 12 bays each side = 208 nails. 13 principal rafters each side × 2 nails each side × 2 nails each = 52.

220 Observed on site, 6 June 2014.

221 Ibid.

222 Geddes 1999, 45, fig 3.8; 52, fig 4.4; 80, fig 4.43; 94, fig 4.93; 182, fig 5.68; and 302.

223 Munby and Steane 1995, 345–6.

224 Worthington and Miles 2006. On tinned nails see Salzman 1952, 308.

225 Thompson 1998, 103–4, 111. In this case the 'smaller' doors, of which there were presumably also two, were probably hung in separate openings, rather than incorporated within the framing of the large ones.

226 For the estimated number of batten nails at 41,250, I am grateful to Dominic Barrington-Groves.

227 Drury McPherson Partnership 2014, 39.

228 WCM 11502.

229 WCM 11501.

230 WCM 11502.

231 WCM 11503; Phillpotts 2010, 29.

232 Phillpotts 2010, 29.

233 D Miles, in preparation.

234 Miles and Haddon-Reece 1995, List 64.

235 Miles and Worthington 2000.

236 Roberts 2011, 59.

237 David Clark and Bob Meeson, pers comm.

238 Peter McCurdy's observation.

239 Stenning 1993, 52 (fig 15) and 75.

240 Austin 1997, 207 (re boarding); Arnold *et al* 2003, 5 (re date); Austin 2005; Canterbury Archaeological Trust; Drury McPherson Partnership 2008, 8.

241 I am grateful to Christopher Dyer for this suggestion.

242 For a detailed account of the recent repair history, *see* Drury McPherson Partnership 2014, 66–72.

243 Ibid, 47.

244 EH file references AA/50817/1A; AA/50817/2.

245 Douglas Rust, pers comm, October 2015.

246 The hatches are not shown by Hartshorne (below, p 65); Drury McPherson Partnership 2014, 66.

247 Drury McPherson Partnership 2014, 79.

248 Estimate and invoices submitted George Ashby Esq, The Close, Harmondsworth by W J Fry Ltd, 30 December 1943 (collection of Gloria Adkin).

249 EH file ref AA50817/2; McVeigh 1979, 29.

250 EH file ref AA50817/2.

251 P B McCurdy to Mike Stock, English Heritage, 22 January 1991.

252 McCurdy 1990.

253 References to the tenants' barns occur for example at SC 2/191/22 and SC 2/191/23 (Court Rolls, 1438, 1439).

254 *See*, for example, Harvey 1976, 12–13.

255 WCM 22091–22093; 22097. *See* p 58.

256 Domesday records 8 hides of demesne. The mid-13th-century custumal describes a demesne-farming regime, and this is implied in the Extents of 1293–4 (NA E101/2/1/), 1324 (NA E 106/7/18 no. 8), and is shown to be the case in the account of that year (NA SC6/1126/5), and from then in numerous documents up to 1450–1. The first Farmer was Robert Iver (WCM 22130).

257 Harvey 1976, 13–14.

258 *VCH Middlesex*, II, 10, 73, 74.

259 Campbell *et al* 1996, 142–77.

260 For example, *see VCH Middlesex*, II, 6 ('the ancient Tithe Barn'); RCHME, 1937, 62 (drawing captioned 'The Tithe Barn at Harmondsworth'; 1950 sales particulars ('the magnificent old TITHE BARN'). On this issue in general, *see* Dyer 1997, 23–5.

261 Brady 1996, 6, 206, 344. *See also* numerous examples cited by Weller 1986, 31, under *Grangia Decimalis*.

262 SC2/191/17 m.22: 'Item quod adhuc *Rogerus Cook non venit ad car(ianda) blada domini cum omnibus suis, et quando venit ad dicta blada domini car(ianda) primam carectatam suam quam car(iavit) proiecit super tassum x^{arum} et alteram carectatam suam proiecit ad unum, et omnes fere garbas dicti bladi fregit et blada disspersit quod nulla carecta potuit in grangiam domini intrare nisi super garbas predictas, ad grave dampnum domini et noc(umentum) bladi domini car(iandi)'*. (And when he came to carry the lord's corn, he flung his first cartload on the tithe heap and he flung his other cartload and he broke all the sheaves of the said corn entirely and dispersed the corn so that no carts were able to enter the grange unless upon the aforesaid sheaves, to the great loss of the lord and to the detriment of carrying the lord's corn.)

263 Christopher Dyer, pers comm, November 2015. *See also* Dyer 2015, 85.

264 *See* Brady 1996, 5–6. Brady's gazetteer contains reference to five tithe barns: the '*grangie pro decimis*' (barn for tithes) noted on the St Paul's manor of Kirby-le-Soken (Essex) in 1335 (p 238), the '*grangiam ad decimas*' (barn for tithes) noted on their manor at Tillingham (Essex) in 1299 (p 252), the barn '*ad reponendum decimas ville*' (for the storing of the tithes of the manor) on their manor of Drayton (Middlesex) in the late 13th or early 14th century (p 344), the '*grangia decimarum*' (barn of the tithes) at Harmondsworth (Middlesex) mentioned in 1405–6 (p 354) and the barn '*pro blado decime*' (for tithe corn) at Bampton Deanery (Oxon) in 1317 (p 354).

265 Weller 1986, 130, citing Hale; Brady 1996, 63; Oschinsky 1971, 420–1 (*Husbandry*, chapter 5) and 392–3 (*Rules*, chapter 4).

266 WCM 11502: *In dicto coopertore conducto ad cooperiend[um] super magna mullonem de pulsis per v dies ii s vi d. In I suo serviente per idem tempus x d.* (For the said roofer brought for the roofing of the great rick of pulses for five days at 2s 6d. And for his assistant for the same time, 10d.)

267 For example, pers comm Serge Brard, Cernay (Normandy), 1988. *See also* Brady 1996, 65–8.

268 Oschinsky 1971, 394–5 (*Rules*, chapter 6); references to keys and locks for barns in Weller 1986, 39, under *clavis*, and 42 under *serruris*.

269 NA SC12/11/20; SC11/444.

270 Harvey 2000, 31–5; 1976, 16.

271 NA SC6/1126/7 [SP 107–8].

272 Kirby 1892, 455–523.

273 On the date of the *Seneschaucy*, *Walter*, *Rules* and *Husbandry*, *see* Oschinsky 1971, 5–9, 75 192, 201, 144–5.

274 Kirby 1892, 183–97.

275 Chitty 1951, 312. The Steward's role was 'non-statutory' ie, rather curiously, not mentioned in the College Statutes.

276 Shipp 2008, 204.

277 Shipp 2008, 198; Kirby 1892, 484–5 (Statutes, Chapter XI).

278 WCM 22103.

279 Chitty 1951, 313.

280 Chitty 1951, 313; NA SC6/1126/7: '*In prebendo equorum Senescalli clerici et aliorum veniendis pro curia tenenda et aliis negociis faciendis vi buss(elli)*'.

281 WCM 11504.

282 NA SC6/1126/6. He was probably a tenant too, 'Ridyng' appearing as a place name in a late 14th-century rental (NA SC12/11/20).

283 WCM 22079, 22080, 22081, 22082, 22083, 11502, 22084, 22085, 22086, 22087.

284 WCM 22087.

285 WCM 22088, 22312, 22089, 11503.

286 WCM 22090, 22091, 22092, 22093.

287 WCM 22095, 22096, 22097 (re Okebourne), 22098, 22099, 22100, 22313.

288 WCM 22101, 22314, 22315, 22104, 22316, 22317, 22105, 22318, 22319, 22107, 22108, 22109, 22321, 22110, 22322, SC6/1126/7. WCM 22111, 22112, 22113, 22323, 22114, 22324, 22115, 22325, 22116–22122.

289 WCM 22123–22125, 11504, 22126–22130.

290 NA SC6/1126/7: '*Stipend(ii) – In Stipendio ballivi per annum – xls*'.

291 WCM 22103 and WCM 22108; *see* Documents (p 66).

292 WCM 11504.

293 At Bredon the chamber was used by the Reeve, answering to the Bishop of Worcester's Bailiff (Dyer 1997, 26–8); Jordan 2006, 74 and pl 9. On the Great Coxwell chamber *see* Jordan 2006, 84–5.

294 NA SC11/446, Rental of the Manor of Harmondsworth, 7 May 1450.

295 *Seneschaucy*, 43 (Oschinsky 1971, 279); on clerks, see Harvey 1976, 36–40.

296 Dyer 1994, 80.

297 Oschinsky 1971, 94–5; *Seneschaucy*.

298 Coghill 1986, I, 33. In the original the lines read: *Wel koude he kepe a garner and a bynne/There was noon auditor koude on him wynne/Wel wiste he by the droghte and by the reyn/The yeldynge of his seed and of his greyn* (Benson 2008, 33, lines 592–6). It has been recently noted however (Stone 2014) that Chaucer's picture of the Reeve's character and skills were based not on his observation of an individual but on a mixture of stereotype and a reading of treatises such as *The Husbandry*.

299 NA SC6/1126/6.

300 WCM 11502.

301 WCM 11503.

302 NA SC/1126/7.

303 WCM 11505.

304 *Seneschaucy*, chapter 4 (Oschinsky 1971, 281).

305 WCM 22087 (*Messorius*).

306 WCM 11504: '*bedell(us) quam simul est messor(ius)*'.

307 NA SC6/1126/7.

308 WCM 11502.

309 WCM 11503: '*De stipend(io) 1 ripereve nichil hoc anno quia nullus est ibidem*' 'reap-reeve' and hayward may sometimes have been synonymous (Harvey 1976, 795.

310 WCM 11502 [SP p 71]. On the office and duties of the reeve see Oschinsky 1971, 94–5; *Seneschaucy* chapters 35, 36, 38 (ibid, 275 and 277).

311 *See* Oschinsky 1971, 167.

312 WCM 11503.

313 NA SC6/1126/7.

314 WCM 11503.

315 Campbell 2000, 218; Titow 1972, 7, describes *curallum* as 'poor quality grain separated mechanically from the better sort of grain'.

316 WCM 11503: '*Et totam dabatur porc(is) hogett(is) porcell(is) et

pulletr(is) necnon columbell(is) in hieme'.

317 I am grateful to Christopher Dyer for advice on this point.

318 Campbell 2000, 227–8.

319 WCM 11504.

320 Dyer 1994, chapter 5, esp 85.

321 Christopher Dyer, pers comm, November 2015: one qr of malt produced 60 gallons of ale.

322 WCM 11503: '*In v ulnis panni linei empt(is) ad fac(iendum) i mappam mensal(ibus) ii 2d*'.

323 WCM 11502; WCM 11503; NA SC/1126/7 '*lxxvii operibus cariac(ionis) bladi proven(ientis) de predict(is) xxxviii virg(atoris) et xxxix semivirg(atoris) quorum quilibet carecta habens cariabit iii carect(as) bladi de camp(is) domini usque in grang(ia) domini nichil pro eodem percipiendo nec pro se nec pro equis suis. Et si quis ill(orum) carectam non habuerit tassabit iii carect(as) bladi in grangia domini*'.

324 I am grateful to Christopher Dyer for advice on this point.

325 Letts 1999, 24–5; Goodall 2012, 81–2, 94–100; Middleton 1798, 172, 183, 188.

326 *Husbandry*, chapter 8 (Oschinsky 1971, 420–1, 422–3).

327 Horn and Born 1979, 359; Hale 1858: '*frumenti ab ostio versus orientem et ab ostio versus occidentem plenum avena. Medietas contra ostium debet esse vacua*'.

328 Horn and Born 1979, 366 and fig 8, 367; Hale 1858.

329 Stacy 2001, 185–6.

330 *See*, for example, the *Husbandry*, chapter 15 (Oschinsky 1971, 424).

331 Hobsbawm and Rudé 1969.

332 *See*, for example, Ambrogio Lorenzetti's *The Effects of Good Government on the Countryside*, painted in the 1330s, showing two pairs of threshers at work, in the open air, during the harvest.

333 *Rules*, chapter 9, Oschinsky 1971, 397.

334 Collins 1972, 32 n6.

335 *Husbandry* (Oschinsky 1971, 424): '*E auxsi deyt hom batre le quarter de

furment e de segle pur iid , e vi quarter de orge, e de feves, e de peys pur id.'

336 I am most grateful to Gergely Rodrics for advice on this point.

337 *See*, for example, the large collection at the Museum of English Rural Life (MERL) Reading.

338 https://www.youtube.com/watch?v=Yzy2VAv-cxM. Film 9, Cséplés Kézicsépléssel, Hungarian Ethnographic Museum (Néprajzi Múzeum). Youtube link kindly supplied by Gergely Rodrics. Accessed 2015.

339 Middleton 1798, 174.

340 Letts 1999, 25.

341 As loosely described, for example, in the *Seneschaucy* (chapter 38, Oschinsky 1971, 276–7).

342 WCM 11504 (SP 118).

343 WCM 78.

344 Collins 1972, 21.

345 *Seneschaucy*, chapter 54 (Oschinsky 1971, 282).

346 *Seneschaucy*, chapters 69; *Husbandry*, chapter 13 (Oschinsky 1971, 288–9 and 424–5). Re dairymaids, *see also* Harvey 1976, 54, n121.

347 *Seneschaucy*, chapter 38 (Oschinsky 1971, 276): '*E prenge garde le prevost, ke nul batur, ne nule ventresse ne prengne del ble pur aporter en seyn, ne en huise, ne en soulers, ne en burse pantenere, ne en sak, ne en sakelet musce pres de la grange.*'

348 A bushel of grain averages 64lb in weight (there are 2,240lb in a ton).

349 Oschinsky 1971, 169.

350 Ibid, 167.

351 Ibid, 168–71.

352 Ibid, 277, with minor changes in translation by Edward Impey: '*E nul cumble de blee ne seyt mes recue de grange en garner pur acreis fere, mes de viii quarters seit pris le ix me de tascurs par dreite mesure pur les acreis, ensy ke nul bussel, ne nul demy bussel, ne nul cantel ne remeyne al provost par lez baturs dehors la mesure avantdite*'.

353 WCM 11501.

354 NA SC6/1126/7.

355 Oschinsky 1971, 323.

356 Clark 2001, 4–5; Campbell *et al* 1993, 60.

357 Oschinsky 1971, 172, 325.

358 Ibid, 174–5.

359 Campbell *et al* 1993, 95–6.

360 Ibid, 61, fig 7, 111.

361 Ibid, 115.

362 Ibid, 53.

363 Ibid, 54, 78.

364 Ibid, 49, 175.

365 Ibid, 110

366 Ibid, 28. The 'Devil's Highway' was the Roman road from Silchester to London.

367 Ibid, 60. These figures apply to the period *c* 1300; on cart hire, *see* Campbell *et al* 1993, 58–9.

368 Ibid, 58.

369 Ibid, 59.

370 Ibid, 24.

371 Ibid, 116.

372 Oschinsky 1971, 396.

373 NA SC6/1126/7: '*De stramine nichil hoc anno vend(ito)*'. (Concerning straw, nothing sold this year.)

374 *VCH Middlesex*, II, 74–5.

375 *VCH Middlesex*, II, 80–1.

376 *VCH Middlesex*, II, 81; *Cal Pat Rolls* 1272–81, 166.

377 On these issues in general, *see* Dyer 2002, 180–2.

378 *VCH Middlesex*, II, 82.

379 *VCH Middlesex*, II, 84.

380 Pevsner 1966, *Berkshire*, 117: 'the largest anywhere'; the *Oxfordshire Villages* website describes Great Coxwell as 'the finest … medieval barn in the country'; the barn at Place Farm, Tisbury (Wiltshire) is described by Pevsner and Cherry 1975, *Wiltshire*, 523, as 'the largest (although not the longest) barn in England, nearly 200ft long'.

381 English Heritage Business Case for the Acquisition of Manor Farm Barn Harmondsworth (Harmondsworth Barn), July 2011.

382 Aston 2000, 168 and fig 106. The length is as measured off the very small published plan. The authors are grateful to Dr Grahame Soffe and Dr Andrew Millard for advice on this site.

383 Impey and Belford 2017.

384 Miles and Haddon-Reece 1995, List 64.

385 Alcock and Tyers 2013, 101. The authors are grateful to Mr Ted Thibaut and other residents of the converted barn for access to the building.

386 Dryden 1897, 187.

387 Horn and Born 1965, 66–7.

388 Aston 2000, 125–6.

389 Bond 2004, 131–2.

390 Bond and Weller 1991, 83; Brady 1996, 117–21.

391 Brady 1996, 117–21 and fig 16, p 120.

392 Including Perrières (Orne), Ardenne (Calvados), and Bretteville-sur-Odon (Calvados), St Wandrille (Seine-Maritime), Maubuisson (Seine-et-Oise), Vaulerent (Seine-et-Oise), Fourcheret, Troussures, and Fay (Oise).

393 Horn 1963.

394 Illustrated in Kirk 1994, 23, fig 13.

395 Nuytten 2005; Horn and Born 1968; Blary 1989, 105–23; Higounet 1965. Blary (p 109) and Higounet (p 8) give dimensions of 72m × 23m: Horn and Born (p 29) give 66.75m × 20.12m, presumably internal.

396 Weller 1986, 27, under *Garderoba*.

397 *See* Bond 2004, 134.

398 Brady 1996, 178–81 for his criteria for inclusion and sample area.

399 On the Winterbourne barn, *see* Miles 2001 and Hall 1980.

400 Campbell 2000, 33.

401 Campbell 2000, 2 and 31.

402 P D A Harvey, 1972, 175.

403 For example, Dyer 1989, 89–91; Postan 1967.

404 WCM 22111: *In dat(is) cuidam carpentar(io) de Woxbrygg' venient(i) ad collegium eodem mense pro convencione faciend(o) cum custode de Nova Grangia faciend(a) apud Hermondeswothe – xx d. In expen(siis) Johannis Godewyn equitant(i) ad Hermond(esworth) pro pecunia querenda eiusdem mense ultra expens(as) alloc(atas) eidem in billa Rogeri Huberd iiii d. Et solut(is) pro expen(siis) Roberti Vyport et aliorum*

*equitanc(ium) ad Hermond(esworth)
mense Julii et fidemissoribus
habend(is) de convencione facta inter
custod(em) et carpentar(ium) pro
I nova grangia ibidem faciend(a)
xiiii s vi d ob. In solucione Johann(is)
Lorimer pro I equo conducto per
iiii dies pro domino Roberto Vyport
equitant(o) cum custod(e) eodem
tempore xvi d.*

405 Berger 1970, 45–6, 125.

406 LMA Acc 0446/ED/164.

407 LMA Acc 0446/ED/151: 'except
and allwaies reserved to the said
Lettice Paget her heirs and assignees,
one barn standing and being at the
northwest end of the Parsonage barne
of Harmondsworth'.

408 Paul Drury's observation (*Conservation
Management Plan*, 2014, 46). The
engraving was made for Cadell and
Davies in 1796, based on an original
probably by Samuel Lysons, pasted
into the grangerised 11-volume edition
of Daniel Lysons' *Environs of London*,
1800, vol V, 142 held by the London
Metropolitan Archive (SC/GL/LYS no.
k1248156).

409 LMA Acc0446/ED/152.

410 WCM 22151: '*pro diversis edificiis de
novo ibidem faciend(is) iii s ii d*' and
'*in liberatis ad construccione(m) Novi
Edificii in manerio de Hermondesworth
hoc anno xli li xviii s vi d.*'

411 Kirby 1903, 357.

412 Thorne 1876, 320; Jerrold 1909, 186.

413 London Metropolitan Archives, Lysons'
*Environs of London Collection (Ref
SC/GL/LYS), vol V, 138; catalogue no
k1248274).

414 Drury McPherson Partnership 2014, 49.

415 WCM 11393, WCM 11394.

416 *VCH Middlesex*, II, 75.

417 WCM 22125.

418 WCM 22132.

419 WCM 11504: '*quod custumarii
noluerunt facere custumali hoc anno*'.

420 WCM 11504: '*quod custumari[ii]
contradicunt cariare hoc anno*'.

421 *See*, for example, Harvey 1991, esp
73–130.

422 Kirby 1903, 37; Kirby 1892, 212;
Mowl 1988, 22; *VCH Middlesex*, II,
75.

423 WCM 22091–22093; WCM 22097.

424 It is possible, though, that *firmarius*
was used in error for *ballivus* or
serviens. I am grateful to Mark Bailey
for advice on this point.

425 WCM 22128.

426 WCM 22130. Iver had previously been
a recalcitrant customary tenant (*VCH
Middlesex*, II, 75).

427 NA E315/463.

428 NA SC6/HenVIII/2105 and NA
C66/729 m.18; Kirby 1892, 251–6.

429 Kirby 1892, 254.

430 Ibid, 251.

431 Thurley 2003, 71.

432 *Cal Pat Rolls* Edward VI, vol I, AD
1547–8, 45.

433 *Dictionary of National Biography*, **42**,
379.

434 Ibid, 354.

435 NA E178/1430.

436 LMA Acc 0446/ED/151.

437 LMA Acc 0446/ED/152.

438 LMA Acc 0446/ED/156.

439 LMA Acc 0446/ED/162.

440 Sherlock 1991, 9–10.

441 LMA Acc 0446/ED/164.

442 Stafford Record Office D603/B/11/2.

443 LMA Acc 0446/ED/162.

444 PROB 11/1258/110; *Journal of
the House of Commons from the
November the 10th 1788 to December
10th 1790*, vol 44, p 156. Hazel
Basford, pers comm.

445 *Dictionary of National Biography*, **2**,
229; **42**, 357.

446 Thorne 1876, 319–20: 'a century back
much larger. It then had a projecting
wing at the N. end so as to form an
L. This wing was taken down about
the same time as the Manor House by
which it stood, and rebuilt at Heath
Row. This, which resembles the
Manor Barn in structure, except that
the walls are of brick, and of course
modern – the oak columns and roof
are the originals. It is 128 feet long and
38 wide'.

447 *VCH Middlesex*, IV, 8; Drury and
McPherson Partnership 2014, 48–9.

448 As shown by the 1894 6in OS map.

449 Springall 1907, 206.

450 Easton and Hodgkinson 2013, and
Easton forthcoming; Easton 2016,
61–2.

451 Foot 1794, 11, 22.

452 Foot 1794, 29.

453 Hazel Basford, pers comm.

454 Wild 2006, 27, citing LMA MR/
DEA/12/Harm.

455 *VCH Middlesex*, IV, 13.

456 Wild 2006, 27.

457 Ibid.

458 *VCH Middlesex*, IV, 13.

459 Drury and McPherson Partnership
2014, 57; Bowlt 2014.

460 The house had certainly been
completed by 1835 as it appears on the
map of that date (Quex Park archives,
kindly supplied by Hazel Basford).

461 Survey of the environs of Manor
Farm, 1830 (Powell-Cotton Museum,
Quex Park), kindly supplied by Hazel
Basford; Drury McPherson Partnership
2014, 58.

462 Collins 1972, 16.

463 Middleton 1798, 173, 183, 192.

464 Hobsbawm and Rudé 1969, 360;
Collins 1972, 19.

465 Hazel Basford, pers comm.

466 Drury and McPherson Associates
2014, 65.

467 Gloria Adkin, nee Ashby, pers comm,
August 2016.

468 *VCH Middlesex*, IV, 13. Mr H E Purser
informed Gillian Wyld, author of the
VCH entry on Harmondsworth in 1960
that 'a little wheat and barley were still
grown'.

469 Sale Particulars, kindly supplied by
Justine Bayley.

470 Drury McPherson Associates 2014, 69.

471 Pearce 1989, 159–60.

472 Drury McPherson Associates 2014, 71.

473 EH Site Management Report – details
of visit 16 March 1995.

474 Reference SD/o5/Arch 7.

475 Nigel Barker, pers comm.

476 Nigel Barker, pers comm.

477 English Heritage Business Case for the Acquisition of Manor Farm Barn Harmondsworth (Harmondsworth Barn), July 2011, 4; Lyndsay Summerfield pers comm.

478 AA 050817/1 (John Tallantyre to Russell Man, 19.10.2009).

479 Under Section 48 of the Planning (Listed Buildings and Conservation Areas Act) 1990.

480 English Heritage Business Case for the Acquisition of Manor Farm Barn, Harmondsworth (Harmondsworth Barn), July 2011, 5.

481 Deborah Lamb to Nigel Barker, Edward Impey and others, 4 August 2011.

482 Sam Foley to Keith Harrison, 1 September 2011.

483 Ceri Pemberton to Liz Rhodes, 25 October 2011.

484 Airports Commission 2015, 30, 34, 99 (fig 5.2) [section 9.141, p 210].

485 Airports Commission 2015, section 9.141, p 210: 'Although the quality of listed buildings lost is highest at Gatwick, the overall impact of is likely to be greatest for the Northwest Runway, where many of the listed buildings are concentrated in the Conservation Area at Longford, which would be removed in its entirety, and Harmondsworth, part of which would be lost. There would also be impacts on the setting of other remaining assets such as Grade I listed Harmondsworth Great Barn, which would sit immediately outside the boundary of the expanded airport, though

486 demolition would not be required'.

486 Drury McPherson Partnership 2014, 102, para 4.8.5.

487 Lysons 1800, 139 (barn) and 142 (church); Britton et al, 1801–18, X, part iv, 623.

488 LMA SC/GL/LYS no. k1248274.

489 Skinner 2010, 250–1. The drawings are held by the RIBA (SKB283/4).

490 Image kindly supplied by Douglas Rust (whereabouts of original unknown). The view is of the interior looking north.

491 Scott 1857, 133.

492 Scott 1879, 262.

493 Morris 1913, xxxii.

494 Scott 1857, 133: 'There is a noble one [barn] at Harmondsworth, in Middlesex, which shews the same type [ie aisled] carried out in timber'. Lochhead 1991, 1.

495 Skinner 2010, 247 and fig 2; Lochhead 1991, 1–2.

496 Lochhead 1999, 23, 68.

497 Cole 1980, 190, n16.

498 On Champney's admiration for Wykeham, see Champney 1888, 161–5, and for his dynastic claim, 165. The link between Mansfield and Harmondsworth is suggested by Watkin 1989, 31.

499 Lethaby 1924, 1. I am grateful to Ruth Whiting for advice on this point. For designs and photographs, see Lethaby 1924, pls 11–14.

500 Cole 1980, 233.

501 Pevsner and Cherry 1973, 165 (Cottingham) and 429 (Thorpe Mandeville).

502 Winchester College Archives, uncatalogued.

503 Hartshorne 1873, 417.

504 For medieval barns destroyed by fire, see Charles et al 1997, v, and see Charles and Horn 1983, 214.

505 Briggs 1934, 218.

506 RCHME 1937, 62.

507 AA 50817/1 (Patrick Duff to Messrs Percy Gore Sons & Co, 15 September 1936). The monument had been 'approved for Scheduling by the Ancient Monuments Board for England on 20 May 1936 (AA 50817/1). (The owner was then Major Percy Henry Gordon Powell-Cotton, Quex Park, Birchington; the tenant was Stanley Bateman, Manor Farm, Harmondsworth.)

508 1 March 1950.

509 Mee 1940, 93.

510 Pevsner 1951, 15.

511 Jenkins 1993, 66–7.

512 In this document the measurement is expressed as v'ga, ie yard. Worth noting, however, is that in relation to the repeat gift in 1430–1 (WCM 22108) the measurement was written virgat', the omission mark standing for the a of virgata, ie a rod (16ft 6in) – a more useful length. However, as Christopher Dyer has pointed out (pers comm 2016), the price of approximately 24d (it was 22d in 1430–1) is standard for a yard of good-quality cloth, suggesting that the second entry was incorrect and that the gift was indeed of one yard.

513 Salzman 1952, 195.

Bibliography

Airports Commission 2015 *Airports Commission: Final Report*. London: Airports Commission

Alcock, N and Tyers, C 2013 'Tree-ring date lists 2013'. *Vernacular Architecture* **44**, 82–111

Alcock, N and Tyers, C 2014 'Tree-ring date lists 2014'. *Vernacular Architecture* **45**, 98–126

Andrews, D D (ed) 1993 *Cressing Temple. A Templar and Hospitaller Manor in Essex*. Chelmsford: Essex County Council

Andrews, F B 1900 'Medieval or "tithe" barns'. *Birmingham Archaeological Society Transactions* **26**, 10–32

Arnold, A J and Howard, R 2016 'The tithe barn, Place Farm, Tisbury Wiltshire. Tree-ring analysis of timbers'. Sherwood: The Nottingham Tree-Ring Dating Laboratory

Arnold, A J, Laxton, R R and Litton, C D 2002 'Tree-ring analysis of timbers from Manor Farm Barn, Frindsbury, Kent'. English Heritage Centre for Archaeology Report 42/2002

Arnold, J, Howard, R E and Litton, C D 2003 'Tree-ring analysis of timbers from Littlebourne Barn, near Canterbury, Kent'. English Heritage Centre for Archaeology Report 95/2003

Aston, M 2000 *Monasteries in the Landscape*. Stroud: Tempus

Austin, R W 1997 'An architectural survey of Littlebourne barn'. *Archaeologia Cantiana* **116**, 203–19

Austin, R W 2005 'Manor Farm Barn, Frindsbury, Kent. An architectural description'. Unpublished report

Bates, D 1988 *Regesta Regum Anglo-Normannorum. The Acta of William I*. Oxford: Clarendon Press

Benson, L D (ed) 2008 *The Riverside Chaucer*. Oxford: Oxford Paperbacks

Berger, R (ed) 1970 *Scientific Methods in Medieval Archaeology*, UCLA Center for Medieval and Renaissance Studies. Berkeley and London: University of California Press

Blary, F 1989 *Le Domaine de Chaalis XIIe–XIVe siècles. Approches archéologiques des établissments agricoles et industriels d'une abbaye cistercienne*. Paris: Editions du CTHS

Blomefield, F 1805–10 *An Essay Towards A Topographical History of the County of Norfolk*, 11 vols. London: W Miller

Bond, C J 1973 'The estates of Evesham Abbey: a preliminary study of their medieval topography'. *Vale of Evesham Historical Society Research Papers* **4**, 1–61

Bond, C J 2004 *Monastic Landscapes*. Stroud: Tempus

Bond, C J and Weller, J 1991 'The Somerset barns of Glastonbury Abbey', *in* L Abrams and J Carley *The Archaeology and History of Glastonbury Abbey. Essays in Honour of the Ninetieth Birthday of C A Ralegh Radford*. Woodbridge: Boydell Press, 57–87

Bowlt, C 2014 'Harmondsworth Manor Farm's other buildings'. *London Archaeologist* **13**(11), Winter 2013/14, 294–8

Brady, N D K 1996 'The sacred barn. Barn-building in southern England, 1100–1550: a study of grain storage technology and its cultural context'. PhD thesis, Cornell University

Brady, N D K 1997 'The gothic barn of England: icon of prestige and authority', *in* E Smith and M Wolfe (eds) *Technology and Resource Use in Medieval Europe: Cathedrals, Mills and Mines*. Aldershot: Ashgate, 76–105

Brayley, E, Brewer, J, and Nightingale, J 1816 *A Topographical and Historical Description of London and Middlesex*, 5 vols. London

Britton, J, Brayley, E, Brewer, J *et al* 1801–18, *The Beauties of England and Wales: or, original delineations, topographical historical and descriptive, of each county: embellished with engravings*, 26 vols. London

Briggs, M 1934 *Middlesex Old and New*. London: George Allen & Unwin

Brown, T 1794 *General View of the Agriculture of the County of Derby, with Observations on the Means of its Improvement*. London

Campbell, B M S 2000 *English Seigniorial Agriculture, 1250–1450*. Cambridge: Cambridge University Press

Campbell, B, Galloway, J, Keene, D, and Murphy, M 1993 *A Medieval Capital and its Grain Supply: Agrarian Production and Distribution in the London Region* c *1300*. Historical Geography Research Series 30. London: Institute of British Geographers

Campbell, B M S, Bartley, K and Power, J P 1996 'The demesne farming systems of post-Black Death England: a classification'. *Agricultural History Review* **44**(2), 131–79

Cazenave, E 1973 'Architecture monastique: les bâtiments utilitaires, les granges du Moyen-Âge dans le département du Calvados'. Masters thesis, Univ Paris IV: Sorbonne

Champneys, B 1888 'William of Wykeham'. *The Art Journal* (June), 161–5

Charles, F W B with Dyer, C and Charles, M 1997 *The Great Barn of Bredon: Its Fire and Rebuilding*. Oxford: Oxbow

Charles, F W B and Horn, W 1966 'The cruck-built barn of Middle Littleton in Worcestershire, England'. *Journal of the Society of Architectural Historians* **25**, 221–39

Charles, F W B and Horn, W 1973 'The cruck-built barn of Leigh Court, Worcestershire, England'. *Journal of the Society of Architectural Historians* **32**, 5–29

Charles, F W B and Horn, W 1983 'The cruck-built barn of Frocester in Gloucestershire'. *Journal of the Society of Architectural Historians* **42**, 211–37

Charpillon, L-E 1868, 1879 *Dictionnaire Historique de Toutes les Communes de l'Eure*, 2 vols. Les Andelys

Chevalier, B 1995 'Un grand domaine agricole de Marmoutier: la Grange de Meslay (IXe–XVIIIe) siècle', *in* E Mornet (ed) *Campagnes Médiévales: l'Homme et son Espace. Etudes Offertes à Robert Fossier*. Paris: Publications de la Sorbonne, 587–60

Chevrefils-Desbiolles, Y 2007 *L'Abbaye d'Ardenne. Histoires du XIIe au XXe siècle*, Paris: IMEC éditeur

Chitty, H 1951 'Stewards of the College Manors'. *The Wykehamist* **977**, 17 October 1951, 312–13

Clark, G 2001 'Markets and economic growth: the grain market of medieval England', unpublished paper

Coghill, N 1986 *The Canterbury Tales*, translated into modern English, 2 vols, London: Century

Cole, D 1980 *The Work of Sir Gilbert Scott*. London: Architectural Press

Collins, E J T 1972 'The diffusion of the threshing machine in England, 1790–1880'. *Tools and Tillage* **2**, 16–33

Cowie, R 2014 'The medieval archaeology of Manor Farm, Harmondsworth, London, Borough of Hillingdon. Project Design for analysis and publication, February 2014'

Davis, V 2007 *William Wykeham*. London: Hambledon Continuum

Decaëns, H 2003 *Histoire de Rouen*. Paris: Editions Jean-Paul Gisserot

De Caumont, A 1846–59 *Statistique Monumental de Calvados*, 4 vols. Caen

Deville, A 1840 'Cartulaire de l'Abbaye de la Sainte-Trinité du Mont de Rouen'. Appendix to M Guérard, *Cartulaire de l'Abbaye de Saint-Bertin*. Paris, 403–87

Dietrich, A and Gaultier, M 2001 'La charpente de la grange abbatiale de Maubuisson (Saint-Ouen-L'Aumône, Val d'Oise'. *Archéologie Médiévale* **30–3** (2000–01), 109–32

Drury McPherson Partnership 2008 *Manor Farm Barn, Findsbury, Conservation Statement*. Consultation Draft

Drury McPherson Partnership 2014 *Manor Farm Barn, Harmondsworth, London Borough of Hillingdon, Conservation Management Plan*

Dryden, H E L 1897 'Two barns at Peterborough formerly belonging to the Abbey'. *Associated Architectural Societies' Reports and Papers* **24**, part I, 177–87

DuCange, Charles du Fresne, and G A Louis Heschel 1840–50 *Glossarium ad scriptores mediae et infimae latinitatis*, 7 vols, Paris: Didot

Dyer, C 1989 *Standards of Living in the Later Middle Ages. Social Change in England* c *1200–1520*. Cambridge: Cambridge University Press

Dyer, C 1994 *Everyday Life in Medieval England*. London and Rio Grande: Hambledon Continuum

Dyer, C 1997 'Bredon barn in history', *in* F W B Charles, *The Great Barn of Bredon: Its Fire and Rebuilding*. Oxford: Oxbow, 23–8

Dyer, C 2002 *Making a Living in the Middle Ages. The People of Britain 850–1520*. New Haven and London: Yale University Press

Dyer, C 2012 'The late medieval village of Wharram Percy: farming the land', *in* S Wrathmell (ed), *A History of Wharram and its Neighbours*. **York:** York University Archaeological Publications, 312–26

Dyer, C 2015 'Peasant farming in late medieval England: evidence from tithe estimations by Worcester Cathedral Priory', *in* M Kowaleski, J Langdon and P Schofield *Peasants and Lords in the Medieval English Economy*. Turnhout: Brepols, 83–109

Easton, T 2016 'Apotropaic symbols and other measures for protecting buildings against misfortune', *in* R Hutton (ed) 2016 *Physical Evidence for Ritual Acts, Sorcery and Witchcraft in Christian Britain*. Basingstoke: Palgrave Macmillan, 39–67

Easton, T forthcoming 'Protective circular symbols in agricultural buildings and stables: a Suffolk study with national implications'. *Historic Farm Buildings Group Journal* no 16

Easton, T and Hodgkinson, J 2013 'Apotropaic symbols on cast-iron firebacks'. *Journal of the Antique Metalware Society* **21**, 14–33

Epaud F 2011 *De la charpente romane à la charpente gothique en Normandie*. Caen: CRAHM

Evans, T A R and Faith, R 1992 'College estates and university finances 1350–1500' *in* J Catto and R Evans (eds) *The History of the University of Oxford*. Oxford: Oxford University Press, 635–706

Farrer, W and Clay, C T 1914–65 *Early Yorkshire Charters: Being a Collection of Documents Anterior to the 13th Century, Made from the Public Records, Monastic Chartularies, Roger Dodsworth's Manuscript and other Available Sources*, 12 vols, Edinburgh

Fletcher, J 1980 'A list of tree-ring dates for building timber in southern England and Wales'. *Vernacular Architecture* **11**, 32–8

Fletcher, J, Tapper, M, and Morris, J J 1985 'List 17 – Dates by Jon Fletcher, Margaret Tapper and Jan Jenkins Morris (Oxford)'. *Vernacular Architecture*, **16**, 41

Foot, P 1794 *General View of the Agriculture of Middlesex*. London

Geddes, J 1999 *Medieval Decorative Ironwork in England*. London: Rep Res Comm Soc Antiq London **59**

Gee, E A 1952–3, 'Oxford Carpenters 1370–1530'. *Oxoniensia* **17–18**, 112–84

Gies, F and Gies, J 2002 *Life in a Medieval Village,* London: HarperPerennial

Goodall, I H 2012 *Ironwork in Medieval Britain. An Archaeological Study*. London: Society for Medieval Archaeology Monograph 31

Hale, W H 1858 *The Domesday of St Paul's of the year MCCXXII, or Registrum de Visitatione Maneriorum per Robertum Decanum*. London: Camden Society

Hall, L 1980 'Barn at Court Farm, Winterbourne, Avon'. Unpublished report

Hardy, T 1874 *Far From the Madding Crowd*, Penguin Classics edition, R Morgan (ed), London 2000

Harper, C G 1904 *The Hardy Country*. London: Adam and Charles Black

Hartshorne, A 1873 'The Great Barn, Harmondsworth'. *Transactions of the London and Middlesex Archaeological Society*, **4**, 1869–74, 417–18 and figs

Harvey, I M W 1991 *Jack Cade's Rebellion of 1450*. Oxford: Clarendon Press

Harvey, J 1978 *The Perpendicular Style*. London: Batsford

Harvey, J 1987 edition, *English Medieval Architects. A Biographical Dictionary Down to 1550*. Gloucester: Alan Sutton

Harvey, P D A 1972 'Agricultural treatises and manorial accounting in medieval England'. *Agricultural History Review* **20**, 170–82

Harvey, P D A 1976 *Manorial Records of Cuxham, Oxfordshire, c 1200–1359*. Oxfordshire Record Society 50. London: HMSO

Harvey, P D A 2000 *Manorial Records*. British Records Association 5 (2 edn)

Hasted, E 1797–1801 *The History and Topographical Survey of the County of Kent* (2 edn), 12 vols, Canterbury

Heaton, M 2007 'Roof of the Abbey Barn, Abotsbury'. *Proceedings of the Dorset Natural History and Archaeological Society* **128**, 120–3

Hérard, P 1901 *Recherches archéologiques sur les abbayes de l'ancien diocèse de Paris*. Paris

Higounet, C 1965 *La Grange de Vaulerent. Structure et exploitation d'un terroir cistercien de la plaine de France XIIe–XVe siècle*. Paris: SEVPEN

Hobsbawm, E J and Rudé, G 1969 *Captain Swing*. London: Lawrence and Wishart

Horn, W 1963 'The Great Tithe Barn of Cholsey, Berkshire'. *Journal of the Society of Architectural Historians* **22**(1), 13–23

Horn, W and Born, E 1968 'The barn of the Cistercian Grange of Vaulerent, Seine-et-Oise, France', *in* A Kosegarten and P Tigler, *Festschrift Ulrich Middeldorf*. Berlin: de Gruyter, 24–41

Horn, W and Born, E 1979 'The Domesday of St Paul's Cathedral, London. A portrait of manorial architecture in twelfth century England', *in* M H King and W M Stevens, *Saints, Scholars and Heroes: Studies in Medieval Culture in Honour of Charles W. Jones*, 2 vols. Collegeville: University of Minnesota, 2, 343–417

Horn, W and Born, E 1965 *The Barns of the Abbey of Beaulieu at its Granges of Great Coxwell and Beaulieu St Leonards*. Berkeley: University of California Press

Howard, R, Laxton, R R, Litton, C D and Simpson, W G 1985 'Tree-ring dates for buildings in the East Midlands'. *Vernacular Architecture* **16**, 39–41

Howlett, D R *et al* 2009 *Dictionary of Medieval Latin from British Sources*, fasc XII. Oxford: Oxford University Press/British Academy

Hudson Turner, T 1847 untitled. *Archaeological Journal* **4**, 249–51

Huggins, P J 1972 'Waltham Abbey. Monastic grange and outer close excavations 1970–72'. *Transactions of the Essex Archaeology Society*, Ser 3, **4**, 30–127

Hurst, J G 1988 'Rural building in England and Wales: England', *in* H E Hallam (ed), *The Agrarian History of England and Wales, II, 1042–1350*. Cambridge: Cambridge University Press 855–932

Hunt, J 1816 letter printed in *The Gentleman's Magazine* **LXXXVI** (February 1816), 105 and engraving opposite

Impey, E 1991 'The origins and development of non-conventual monastic dependencies in England and Normandy, 1050–1350'. Unpublished DPhil thesis, University of Oxford

Impey, E 2004 'The alien priory of St Winwaloe and Winnold House at Wereham, Norfolk'. *Norfolk Archaeology* **44**, 432–54

Impey, E and Belford, P 2017 'The lost great barn of Abingdon Abbey at Cumnor, Oxon'. *Oxoniensia* **82**

Jenkins, S 1993 'John Betjeman's Heathrow' *in* S Jenkins *The Selling of Mary Davies and Other Writings*. London: John Murray, 63–70

Jerrold, W 1909 *Highways and Byways in Middlesex*. London: Macmillan and Co

Jordan, T 2006 *Cotswold Barns*. Stroud: The History Press

Kirby, T F 1892 *Annals of Winchester College*. London and Winchester: H Frowde

Kirby, T F 1903 'Charters of Harmondsworth, Isleworth, Twickenham and Hampton-on-Thames'. *Archaeologia* **58**, 341–58

Kirk, M 1994 *The Barn. Silent Spaces*. London and New York: Thames and Hudson

Kohnert, T (ed) 2012 *Harmondsworth Great Barn, London*. HAWK Institut Baudenkmalpflege – Projektwoche SoSe

Lethaby, W R 1924 'Ernest Gimson's London Days' *in* W R Lethaby, A H Powell and F L Grigg *Ernest Gimson: His Life and Work*, Stratford-upon-Avon: Shakespeare Head Press, 1–10

Letts, J 1999 *Smoke Blackened Thatch: A Unique Source of Late Medieval Plant Remains from Southern England*. English Heritage/University of Reading

Lochhead, I 1991 *Unbuilt Christchurch, An Exhibition of Architectural Drawings from 1850 to the 1980s* (exhibition catalogue). Christchurch: Christchurch Art Gallery

Lochhead, I 1999 *A Dream of Spires. Benjamin Mountford and the Gothic Revival*. Christchurch: Canterbury University Press

Lysons, D 1800 *An Historical Account of those Parishes in the County of Middlesex which are not included in the Environs of London by the Rev Daniel Lysons*. London

Manwaring Baines, J 1986 *Historic Hastings. A Tapestry of Life*, rev edn. St Leonards-On-Sea: Cinque Port

Matthew, D 1962 *The Norman Monasteries and their English Possessions*. Oxford: Oxford University Press

McCurdy, P 1990, 'Harmondsworth Manor Barn: timber frame survey drawings', unpublished report

McVeigh, S A J 1979 *Harmondsworth's Glory*. Privately printed

Mee, A 1940 *Middlesex*. London: Hodder & Stoughton

Middleton, John 1798 *View of the Agriculture of Middlesex; with Observations on the Means of its Improvement and Several Essays on Agriculture in General*. London

Miles, D H 2001 *The Tree-Ring Dating of Court Farm Barn, Church Lane, Winterbourne, Gloucestershire*. Centre for Archaeology Report 34/2001

Miles, D H 2005 'New developments in the interpretation of dendrochronology as applied to oak buildings'. Unpublished DPhil thesis, University of Oxford

Miles, D and Haddon-Reece, D 1995 List 64 (II) – Tree-ring dates. *Vernacular Architecture* **26**, 62–74 General List

Miles, D H and Worthington, M J 2000 'Tree-ring dates'. *Vernacular Architecture* **31**, 90–113

Morgan, M 1941–2 'The suppression of the alien priories'. *History* **36**, 204–12

Morris, M (ed) 1913 *The Collected Works of William Morris*. London: Longmans, Green and Co

Mowl, T 1988 'The Great Barn at Harmondsworth'. Typescript

Munby, J 1988 'Great Coxwell Barn'. *Archaeological Journal*, supplement to **145**, 73–7

Munby, J, Steane, J *et al* 1995 'Swalcliffe: A New College farm in the fifteenth century'. *Oxoniensia* **60**, 333–78

Newman, J 1995 *The Buildings of Wales: Glamorgan*. London: Penguin Books

Nuytten, D 2005 'Bruges, recherches archéologiques sur l'ancien Grange de Ter Doest'. *Bulletin Monumental* **163**, 157–62

Oschinsky, D (ed) 1971 *Walter of Henley and Other Treatises on Estate Management and Accounting*. Oxford: Oxford University Press

Pathy-Barker, C 1989 'The 1989 Excavations at Manor Court, Harmondsworth'. Museum of London Archaeology. Typescript report, unpaginated

Pearce, D 1989 *Conservation Today*. London and New York

Pevsner, N 1951 *The Buildings of England: Middlesex*. London: Penguin Books

Pevsner, N 1966 *The Buildings of England: Berkshire*. London: Penguin Books

Pevsner, N and Cherry, B 1973 *The Buildings of England: Northamptonshire*. London: Penguin Books

Pevsner, N and Cherry, B 1975 *The Buildings of England: Wiltshire*. London

Phillpotts, C 2010 'Documentary research report (section 22)' *in* J Lewis *et al* 2010 *Landscape Evolution in the Middle Thames Valley. Heathrow Terminal 5 Excavations*, vol 2, Framework Archaeology Monograph **3**

Pommeraye, J F 1662 'Histoire de l'Abbaye de La Tres Sainte Trinité-du-Mont dite depuis de Sainte Catherine du Mont de Rouen' *in Histoire de l'Abbaye Royale de St Ouen*, Rouen

Postan, M M 1967 'Investment in medieval agriculture'. *Journal of Economic History* **27**, 576–87

Rackham, O 1993 'Woodland management and timber economy as evidenced by the buildings at Cressing Temple' *in* D D Andrews (ed) *Cressing Temple. A Templar and Hospitaller Manor in Essex*. Chelmsford: Essex County Council, 85–92

Rigold, S 1979 'The lost barn of Chislet, *in* K H McIntosh, *Chislet and Westbere: Villages of the Stour Lathe*. Canterbury

Roberts, E 2011 'Early roofs in Hampshire: 1240–1600' *in* J Walker (ed) *The English Medieval Roof – Crownpost to Kingpost*. Report of the Essex Historic Buildings Group Day School 2008

Robinson, E and Worssam, B 1989 'The geology of some Middlesex churches'. *Proceedings of the Geologists' Association* **100**(4), 595–603

Royal Commission on Ancient and Historical Monuments in Wales 1982 *An Inventory of the Ancient Monuments in Glamorgan, III, Medieval Secular Monuments, Part II: Non-defensive*. Cardiff: HMSO

Royal Commission on Historical Monuments (England) 1937 *An Inventory of the Historical Monuments in Middlesex*. London: HMSO

Royal Commission on Historical Monuments (England) 1952 *An Inventory of the Historical Monuments in Dorset*, 3 vols, *West*. London: HMSO

Royal Commission on Historical Monuments (England) 1987 *Churches of South-East Wiltshire*. London: HMSO

Salter, H E 1925 'Two deeds of the Abbey of Bec'. *English Historical Review* **40** (January), 73–8

Salzman, L F 1952 *Building in England Down to 1540: A Documentary History*. Oxford: Clarendon Press

Scott, G G 1857 *Remarks on Secular and Domestic Architecture, Present and Future*. London

Scott, G G 1879 *Lectures on the Rise and Development of Mediaeval Architecture*, 2 vols. London

Sherlock, D 1991 *Prior's Hall Barn, Widdington, Essex*. English Heritage Guidebook

Sherwood, P 2009 *Heathrow Airport: 2000 Years of History*. Stroud: The History Press

Shipp, A 2008 'William of Wykeham and the founding of Winchester College'. Unpublished PhD thesis, University of Exeter

Skinner, R 2010 'Drawings from an indigenous tradition? George Gilbert Scott's First Design for Christchurch Cathedral, 1861–62'. *Journal of the Society of Architectural Historians* **53**, 245–70

Slavin, P 2012 *Bread and Ale for the Brethren. The Provisioning of Norwich Cathedral Priory 1260–1535*. Studies in Regional and Local History 11. Hatfield: University of Hertfordshire Press

Slocombe, P M 2016 'Tithe Barn Place Farm Tisbury'. Wiltshire Building Record, Chippenham

Springall, S 1907 *Country Rambles Round Uxbridge. A Descriptive Guide to the Neighbourhood*. Uxbridge

Stacy, N E (ed) 2001 *Surveys of the Estates of Glastonbury Abbey, c 1135–1201*. British Academy Records of Social and Economic History, New Series, 33

Steer, F W 1950 *Farm and Cottage Inventories of Mid Essex, 1635–1749*. Chelmsford: Essex County Council

Stenning, D 1993 'The Cressing barns and the early development of barns in south-east England' *in* D D Andrews (ed) *Cressing Temple. A Templar and Hospitaller Manor in Essex*. Chelmsford: Essex County Council, 51–75

Stone, D 2014 'The Reeve: ideology and meaning' *in* S H Rigby (ed) *Historians on Chaucer. The 'General Prologue' to the Canterbury Tales*. Oxford: Oxford University Press, 399–420

Tabuteau, E Z 1988 *Transfers of Property in Eleventh-Century Norman Law*. London: University of North Carolina Press

Thompson, A, Westman, A and Dyson, T (eds) 1988 *Archaeology in Greater London 1965–90: A Guide to Records of Excavations by the Museum of London*. The Archaeological Gazetteer Series, 2. London: Museum of London

Thompson, M 1998 'The building of a barn, byre and carthouse on Glastonbury Abbey's manor of Street between 1340 and 1343'. *Proceedings of the Somerset Archaeological and Natural History Society* **141**, 103–114

Thorne, J 1876 *Handbook to the Environs of London*, 2 vols. London: John Murray

Thurley, S 2003 *Hampton Court. A Social and Architectural History*. New Haven and London: Yale University Press

Timson, R T (ed) 1973 *The Cartulary of Blyth Priory*, Thoroton Soc Nottinghamshire, Record Ser 27, 28

Titow, J Z 1969 *English Rural Society 1200–1350*. London: Allen and Unwin

Titow, J Z 1972 *Winchester Yields. A Study in Medieval Agricultural Productivity*. Cambridge: Cambridge University Press

Tyers, I 1990 'List 37 – Tree-ring dates'. *Vernacular Architecture* **21**, 45–6

Tyers, I, 1993 'Tree-ring dating at Cressing Temple, and the Essex curve' *in* D D Andrews (ed) *Cressing Temple. A Templar and Hospitaller Manor in Essex*. Chelmsford: Essex County Council, 77–83

Tyers, I 2015 *Manor Farm Barn, Manor Court, High Street, Harmondsworth, London Borough of Hillingdon. Dendrochronological Analysis of Oak Structural Timbers and Boards*. Historic England Research Report Series no 12-2015

Tyers, I and Hibberd, H 1993 'Tree-ring dates from the Museum of London Archaeology Service: List 53'. *Vernacular Architecture* **24**, 50–4

Tyers, I, Groves, C, Hillam, J, and Boswick, G 1997 'List 80 – Tree-ring dates from Sheffield University'. *Vernacular Architecture* **28**, 138–58

Watkin, D 1989 *The Architecture of Basil Champneys*. Cambridge: Newnham College

Weller, J 1986 *Grangia & Orreum. The Medieval Barn: A Nomenclature: An Interim Study with Related Commentaries: The Origins and Use of the Grangia*. Bildeston Booklets, Bildeston

Wild, W 2006 'Enclosure in the 19th century (Part 2)'. *West Middlesex Family History Society Journal* **27**(1), 27–31

Willis, R 1843 *A Description of the Sextry Barn at Ely, Lately Demolished*. London

Wood-Jones, R B 1956 'The rectorial barn at Church Enstone'. *Oxoniensia* **21**, 43–7

Worthington, M and Miles, D 2006 *New College, Oxford: Tree Ring Dating of the Bell-Tower and Cloister Door*. English Heritage Research Department Report Series 56/2006

Acknowledgements

The authors are grateful to many people who have helped with the writing of this monograph and the work on which it is based. Of these, six have made a particularly prominent contribution: Mark Bailey who kindly advised on numerous aspects of the interpretation of the medieval accounts; Christopher Dyer, who read two drafts of the text and has made numerous immensely valuable suggestions and corrections; Richard Lea, for his study of the building's construction sequence and the drawings illustrating it; Stephen Priestley, who transcribed the vast majority of the medieval manuscript material cited here and for advice on points of interpretation; Lyndsay Summerfield of Historic England, for tireless support in organising fieldwork, gathering materials and data, assistance with editing and much else; and Dr Tillman Kohnert for kindly allowing the free use of photographs and graphics prepared for the 2012 report. Among the remainder are Gloria Adkin, Nathaniel Alcock, Paul Backhouse, Justine Bayley, John Blair, François Blary, James Bond, the late Serge Brard, Dominic Barrington-Groves, Hazel Basford, Martin Biddle, Katy Carter, Michael Copeman, Emma Carver, Jean-Paul Corbasson, Andy Crispe, John Crook, Mark Davies, Vincent Debonne, Michael Dunn, Paul Drury, Mark Fenton, Suzanne Foster, Jane Geddes, Ndai Halisch, Jane Impey, Karen Impey, Michael Jones, Robert Jones, Derek Keene, Jon Kiely, Phillip Lane, Yannick Ledigol, Elisabeth Lescroart, Yves Lescroart, Stephen Letch, Ian Lochhead, Clare Loughlin, the late Candida Lycett-Green, Alastair Morrison, Malcom Mercer, Julian Munby, Toby Murphy, Matthew Rice, Bronwen Riley, Thom Richardson, Sebastian Roberts, David Robinson, Gergeley Rodric, Joy Russell, Douglas Rust, Pat Ryan, Christine Toulier, Chris Smith, Grahame Soffe, Tim Tatton-Brown, Simon Thurley, Paula Turner, Sonja Vanblaere, Giles Vilain, Ruth Whiting, and Bernard Worssam.

Index